1

# ScottForesman

## Accelerating English Language Learning

### Authors

Anna Uhl Chamot

Jim Cummins

Carolyn Kessler

J. Michael O'Malley

Lily Wong Fillmore

### Consultant

George González

ScottForesman

Editorial Offices: Glenview, Illinois
Regional Offices: Sunnyvale, California • Atlanta, Georgia
Glenview, Illinois • Oakland, New Jersey • Dallas, Texas

**Illustrations** Unless otherwise acknowledged, all illustrations are the property of Scott, Foresman and Company. Page abbreviations are as follows: (T) top, (B) bottom, (L) left, (R) right, (C) center.

Lisa Adams 62, 72–73; Elizabeth Allen 10–11, 18–19, 39, 40–41, 46, 70–71, 77, 80–81, 102–103, 118–119, 142–143, 180, 186–187, 197, 211; Lee Lee Brazeal 38, 64–65, 204; Ruth Bornstein 26–37; John Burgoyne 104, 105, 208–209; Patrice Rossi Calkin 231; Ruta Daugavietis 138, 233; Paul Dolan 114, 202–203; Bob Dorsey 161; Ebet Dudley 146; Lane DuPont 76; 140–141, 148–149, 194–195; James Endicott 216–227; Lane Gregory 193, 234–235, 236; Yumi Heo 88–99; Todd Leonardo 15; Jill Murphy 164–175; Anita Nelson 86–87, 108–109, 176, 184–185, 206–207, 213; Cheryl Roberts 66–69, 100, 122, 156–157, 190; John Sandford 24–25, 42–43, 83, 84, 120–121, 150–152, 200–201, 228; Janice Skivington 6–9, 44–45, 63; Susan Spellman 16–17, 48–49, 110–111, 116–117, 188–189; Three Communication Design 12–13, 74–75, 115, 123; Elaine Wadsworth 4–5; Nadine Bernard Westcott 126–137.

**Literature** 26-37: Text and selected illustrations from LITTLE GORILLA by Ruth Bornstein. Copyright © 1976 by Ruth Bornstein. All rights reserved. Reprinted by permission of Clarion Books/Houghton Mifflin Company. 50-61: MY SCHOOL, YOUR SCHOOL by Bette Birnbaum. Copyright © 1990 American Teachers Publications. Reprinted by permission of Raintree/Steck-Vaughn Publishers. 88-99: ONE AFTERNOON by Yumi Heo. Copyright © 1994 by Yumi Heo. All rights reserved. Reprinted by permission of Orchard Books, New York. 126-137: From THE LADY WITH THE ALLIGATOR PURSE by Nadine Bernard Westcott. Copyright © 1988 by Nadine Bernard Westcott. Reprinted by permission of Little, Brown and Company. 164-175: From PEACE AT LAST by Jill Murphy. Copyright © 1980 by Jill Murphy. Reprinted by permission of Dial Books for Young Readers, a division of Penguin Books USA Inc. 216-227: TREES by Harry Behn, illustrated by James Endicott. Copyright 1949 by Harry Behn. Copyright © renewed 1977 by Alice L. Behn. Illustrations copyright © 1992 by James Endicott. A Bill Martin Book for Henry Holt and Company. Reprinted by permission of Marian Reiner and Henry Holt and Co., Inc.

**Poems and Songs** 14: "My Baby Brother" from FATHERS, MOTHERS, SISTERS, BROTHERS: A COLLECTION OF FAMILY POEMS by Mary Ann Hoberman. Text copyright © 1991 by Mary Ann Hoberman. Reprinted by permission of Little, Brown and Company. 38: "Everything Grows" Words by Raffi, D. Pike. Music by Raffi. Copyright © 1987 by Homeland Publishing (SOCAN) A division of Troubadour Records Ltd. All rights reserved. Reprinted by permission. 62: From "The First Day of School" by Sarah Wilson. Reprinted by permission of Edythea Ginis Selman Literary Agency Inc. 76: "If You're Happy and You Know It" from SALLY GO ROUND THE SUN by Edith Fowke. Text copyright © 1969 McClelland and Stewart Ltd. Reprinted by permission of McClelland and Stewart Ltd., Canada. 138: "Look Both Ways" by Dee Lillegard from HUMPTY DUMPTY'S MAGAZINE. Copyright © 1984 by Children's Better Health Institute, Benjamin Franklin Literary & Medical Society, Inc., Indianapolis, Indiana. Reprinted by permission. 150-152: "Allie Alligator" by Babs Bell Hajdusiewicz, illustrated by John Sanford from SCOTT FORESMAN HOLISTIC TESTS, Grade 1. Copyright © 1995 ScottForesman and Company. 176: "The Bear Went Over The Mountain" from EYE WINKER TOM TINKER CHIN CHOPPER by Tom Glazer, 1973. Reprinted by permission of Songs Music, Inc. 190: "The Clap and Quiet Poem" from SEPTEMBER TO SEPTEMBER by Dee Lillegard. Copyright © 1986 by Regensteiner Publishing Enterprises, Inc. Published by Childrens Press. Reprinted by permission of Grolier Publishing Co. 204: "You'll Sing A Song And I'll Sing A Song" from THE ELLA JENKINS SONG BOOK FOR CHILDREN. Copyright © 1966 Ella Jenkins. Reprinted by permission of the author. 228: "Shadows" from JUST AROUND THE CORNER by Leland B. Jacobs, Revised Edition. Text copyright © 1993 by Allan D. Jacobs. Reprinted by permission of Henry Holt and Co., Inc.

**Photography** Unless otherwise acknowledged, all photographs are the property of Scott, Foresman and Company. Page abbreviations are as follows: (T) top, (C) center, (B) bottom, (R) right.

v(r) Superstock; v(l) Lawrence Migdale; 2(b), 3(b) Superstock, Inc.; 3(t) Lawrence Migdale; 6–7, 8–9 Courtesy Musem of New Mexico, Photo by Wyatt Davis, Neg. 11567; 14 Superstock, Inc.; 21 Tony Porto; 23(b) National Audubon Society/Photo Researchers; (t) Paul Freed/Animals Animals; 47 Myrleen Ferguson/PhotoEdit; 50, 51 Michael Heron; 52, 54, 55, 56, 57 Lawrence Migdale; 53(t, b) Richard Hutchings/PhotoEdit; 58(t, b) Lea/OMNI-Photo Communications, Inc.; 59(t, b) Michael Heron; 60, 61 Ted Horowitz/Stock Market; 78(t, c), 79(t, b), 106(t, b), 107(t) Superstock, Inc.; 109(t, b) Don & Pat Valenti; 109(c), 112, 125(r) Superstock, Inc.; 125(l) David Young-Wolff/PhotoEdit; 154(bl) Gary Benson/Tony Stone Images; (t) Superstock, Inc.; (br) Jonathan Nourok/PhotoEdit; 158(br,tr), 159(tl, tr) Superstock, Inc.; 179(cr) Don & Pat Valenti; (c l, bl, br) Superstock, Inc.; 181(br) Don & Pat Valenti; 181(tr,bl), 182(bl,cr,cl), 183(tr, bl, br, cr) Superstock, Inc.; 212(t) Mark Lewis/Tony Stone Images; (b) Superstock, Inc.; (c) Photri, Inc.

ISBN: 0-673-19668-2

Copyright © 1997 by Scott, Foresman and Company
A Pearson Education Company.
All Rights Reserved. Printed in the United States of America.

7 8 9 10 KR 05 04 03 02 01 00

# CRITIC READERS

**Sandra H. Bible**
Elementary ESL Teacher
Shawnee Mission School District
Shawnee Mission, Kansas

**Betty A. Billups**
Dallas Independent School District
Dallas, Texas

**María G. Cano**
BIL/ESL Specialist
Pasadena Independent School District
Pasadena, Texas

**Anaida Colón-Muñiz, Ed.D.**
Director of English Language
 Development and Bilingual
 Education
Santa Ana Unified School District
Santa Ana, California

**Debbie Corkey-Corber**
Educational Consultant
Williamsburg, Virginia

**Lily Pham Dam**
Instructional Specialist
Dallas Independent School District
Dallas, Texas

**María Delgado**
Edison Middle School
Milwaukee Public Schools
Milwaukee, Wisconsin

**Dr. M. Viramontes de Marín**
Chair, Education/Liberal Arts
 Departments
The National Hispanic University
San Jose, California

**Timothy Hart**
Supervisor of English as a
 Second Language
Wake County
Raleigh, North Carolina

**Lilian I. Jezik**
Bilingual Resource Teacher
Colorna-Norco Unified School District
Norco, California

**Helen L. Lin**
Chairman, Education Program
Multicultural Arts Council of
 Orange County, California
Formerly ESL Lab Director,
 Kansas City, Kansas, Schools

**Teresa Montaño**
United Teachers Los Angeles
Los Angeles, California

**Loriana M. Novoa, Ed.D.**
Research and Evaluation Consultants
Miami, Florida

**Rosa María Peña**
Austin Independent School District
Austin, Texas

**Thuy Pham-Remmele**
ESL/Bilingual K–12 Specialist
Madison Metropolitan School District
Madison, Wisconsin

**Roberto San Miguel**
Kennedy-Zapata Elementary School
El Cenizo, Texas

**Jacqueline J. Servi Margis**
ESL and Foreign Language
 Curriculum Specialist
Milwaukee Public Schools
Milwaukee, Wisconsin

**Elizabeth Streightoff**
ESL Magnet Teacher,
 Lamar Elementary School
Conroe Independent School District
The Woodlands, Texas

**Lydia M. Trujillo**
Hot Topics Consultants
Pueblo, Colorado

**Susan C. VanLeuven**
Poudre R-1 School District
Fort Collins, Colorado

**Rosaura Villaseñor, M.A.**
Educator
Norwalk, California

**Sharon Weiss**
ESL Consultant
Glenview, Illinois

**Cheryl Wilkinson**
J. O. Davis Elementary School
Irving Independent School District
Irving, Texas

**Phyllis I. Ziegler**
ESL/Bilingual Consultant
New York, New York

# TABLE OF CONTENTS

**CHAPTER 1**

Families .................................................. 2

**CHAPTER 2**

Growing and Changing ....................... 16

**CHAPTER 3**

At School ............................................ 40

**CHAPTER 4**

Learning ............................................. 64

**CHAPTER 5**

Neighbors ........................................... 78

**CHAPTER 6**

Animals and Their Homes ................. 102

**CHAPTER 7** How You Can Feel Safe ..................... 116

**CHAPTER 8** How You Can Feel Healthy ................. 140

**CHAPTER 9** Using Our Senses ............................. 154

**CHAPTER 10** How We See and Hear ...................... 178

**CHAPTER 11** The Four Seasons ............................ 192

**CHAPTER 12** Trees ............................................. 206

Children's Reference Section .............. 230

# CHAPTER 1

# Families

## Tell what you know.

Who is in each **family?**

**Talk About It**

Draw your family.
Describe your
family.

3

# What do families do?

**Word Bank**

care

hug

listen

share

Families eat together.

Families help each other.

Families work and play together.

Family members show they love each other.

**Talk About It**

What does your family do together?

# Work of Long Ago

Some families worked on farms.

They grew plants for food.

They raised animals for food.

**Mothers** made clothes.

Children helped.

**Fathers** made furniture.

Children helped.

 **Draw About It**

How do you help your family?
Draw a picture to show what you do.

# Fun of Long Ago

Families invited friends to visit.

They ate together.

They danced.

**Word Bank**

**dance**

**eat**

**play**

**sing**

 **Talk About It**

What does your family do for fun?

# Peter's family changes.

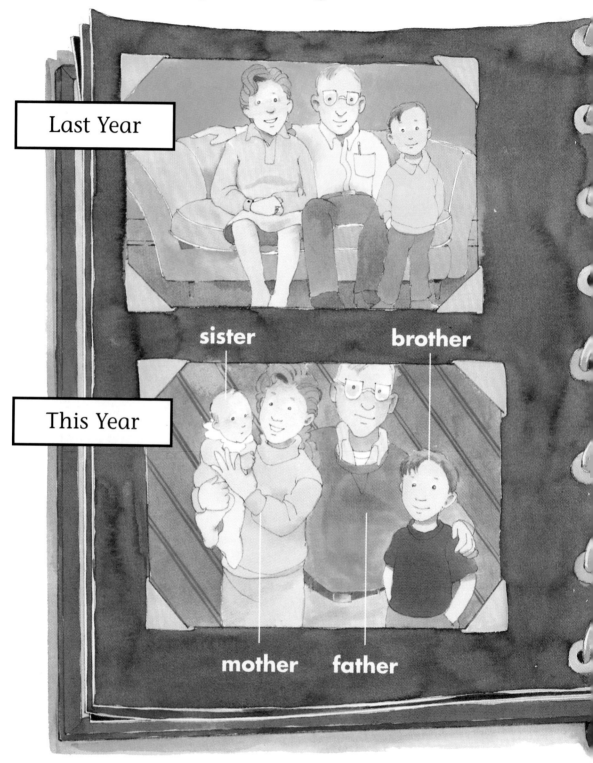

Last Year

This Year

sister

brother

mother

father

# Peter's New Sister

Sometimes Peter plays with his sister.

Sometimes Peter plays with friends.

How is your family growing and changing?

Tell a friend how you have changed since last year.

# My Family

by Juan Castro, age 6

This is my family. This is my father, my mother, Becky, and Pablo.

I have fun at the pool
with my brother.

My family likes to dance.

# My
## Baby Brother

### by Mary Ann Hoberman

My baby brother's beautiful,
So perfect and so tiny.
His skin is soft and velvet brown;
His eyes are dark and shiny.

His hair is black and curled up tight;
His two new teeth are sharp and white.
I like it when he chews his toes;
And when he laughs, his dimple shows.

## Draw About It

Draw a picture of someone in your family.

# Tell what you learned.

**1.** Who is in this family?

**2.** How are they helping each other?

**3.** What do you do with your family? Draw a picture. Tell a friend about your drawing.

# Growing and Changing

# Tell what you know.

How do you know you have grown?

I am **bigger.**

I am **taller.**

# What new things can they do?

He can ride his ▶
bike now.

She can hit a ball. ▲

**Talk About It**

What new things
can you do?

# How do children grow?

When you were a **baby** you were very **small**.

1 year old

2 years old

3 years old

You grew and grew.

4 years old

5 years old

6 years old

Now you are **bigger** and **taller**.

When you were a baby, you could not do many things.

Now you are bigger. You have changed. You can do many things.

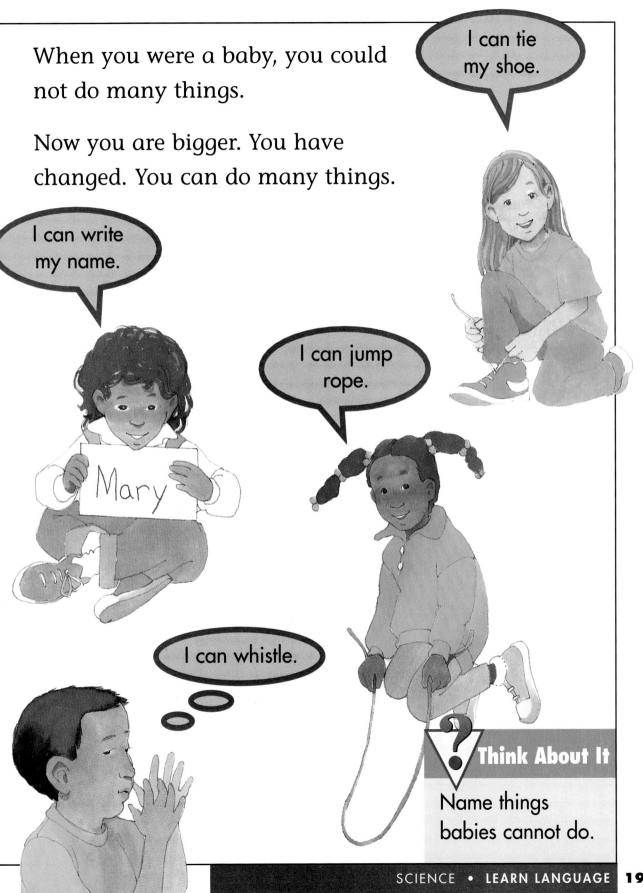

I can tie my shoe.

I can write my name.

Mary

I can jump rope.

I can whistle.

**Think About It**

Name things babies cannot do.

# How big are your hands?

Which hand print is bigger?

Which hand print is smaller?

Find the hand print that is bigger than your hand.

Find the hand print that is smaller than your hand.

# Have your teeth changed?

Kara age 4

Kara age 6

**Draw About It**

Look in a mirror. Smile! Draw what you see.

# Make a home for mealworms.

## Things You Need

tape

apple slice

oatmeal

mealworms

plastic container with lid

## Follow these steps.

**1.** Put some oatmeal into the container.

**2.** Place an apple slice into the container.

**3.** Put mealworms into the container. Tape on the lid.

**4.** Put the home in a warm place away from sunlight.

# Watch mealworms grow and change.

pupa

beetle

## Things You Need

 mealworm home

🔍 hand lens

🖍️ mealworms

🖍️ crayons

## Follow these steps.

**1.** Place a mealworm on a paper.

**2.** Look at the mealworm with the hand lens.

**3.** Watch the mealworm for 14 days. Watch the color, size, and shape change.

 **Draw About It**

Draw two pictures. Show how the mealworms look the first day. Show how the mealworms look the last day.

# Measure animals in the spring.

**Word Bank**

inch

ruler

How long is the turtle?

How long is the yellow fish?

How long is the pink fish?

Use a string to help you measure.

# Measure animals in the fall.

Did the turtle grow longer?

Did the yellow fish grow longer?

Did the pink fish grow longer?

How much did each animal grow?

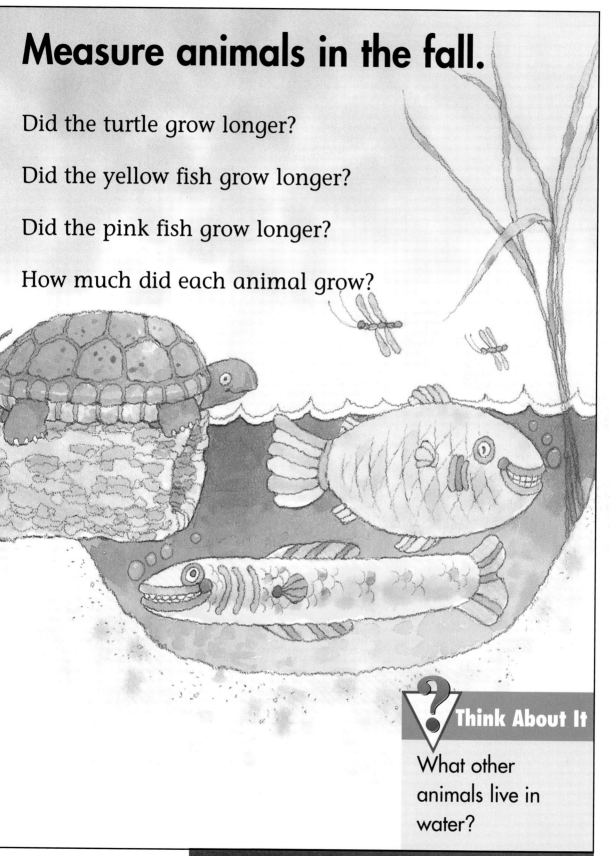

**Think About It**

What other animals live in water?

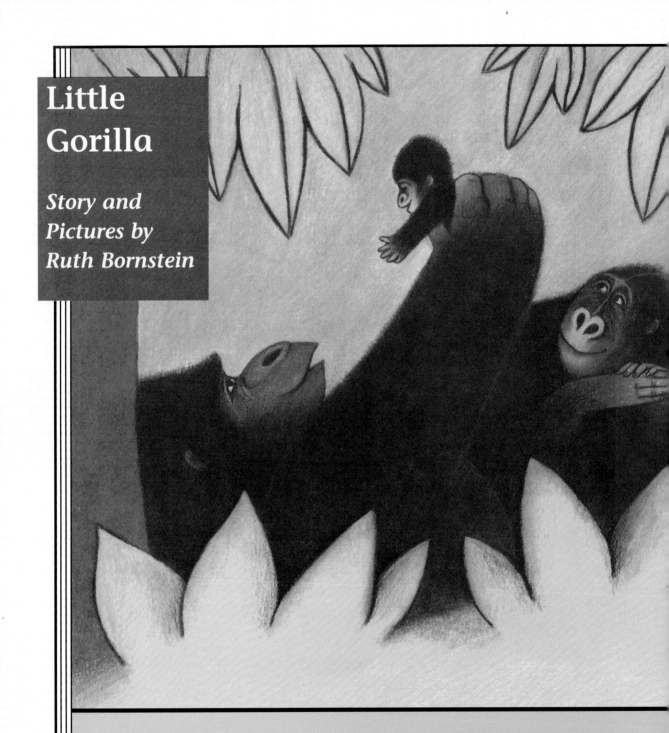

# Little Gorilla

*Story and Pictures by Ruth Bornstein*

Once there was a little gorilla, and everybody loved him. His mother loved him. His father loved him.

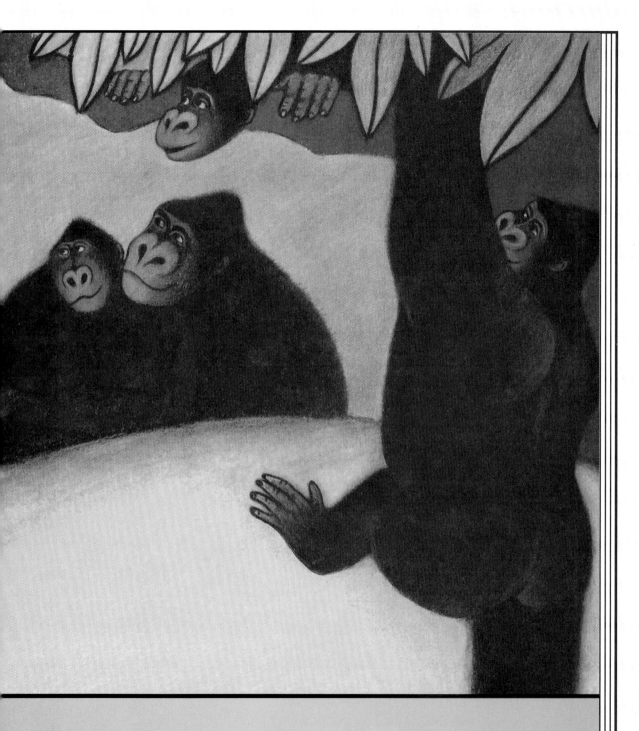

His grandma and grandpa, and his aunts and uncles loved him. Even when he was only one day old, everybody loved Little Gorilla.

Pink Butterfly flying through the forest,

Green Parrot in his tree, and Red Monkey in her tree, all loved Little Gorilla.

Even Big Boa Constrictor thought Little Gorilla was nice.

Giraffe, walking tall through the forest, was there when Little Gorilla needed him. Young Elephant, and Old Elephant too, came to see him.

Lion roared his loudest roar for him. Even Old Hippo took him wherever he wanted to go, because she loved Little Gorilla.

Just about everybody in the great green forest
loved Little Gorilla!

Then one day something happened . . . Little
Gorilla began to grow and Grow

and Grow and GROW. And one day, Little
Gorilla was BIG!

And everybody came, and everybody sang
"Happy Birthday Little Gorilla!"

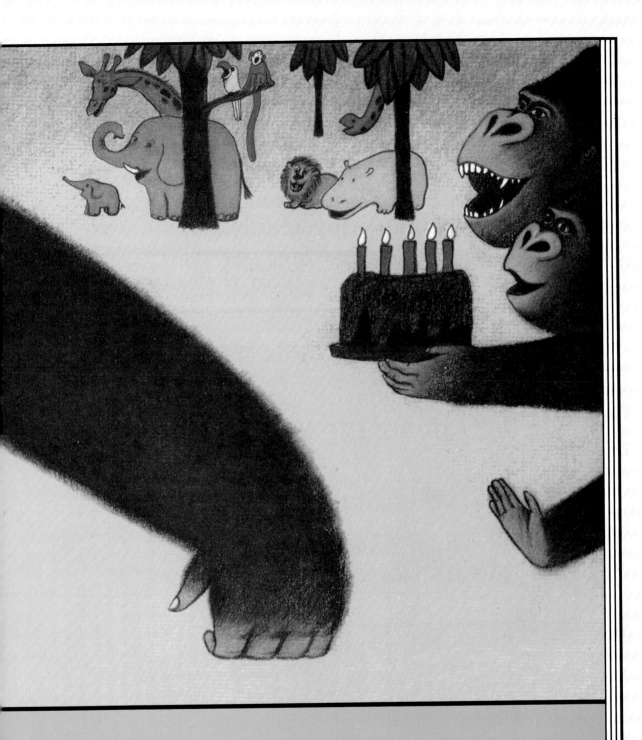

And everybody still loved him.

# Everything Grows

**by Raffi**

Everything grows and grows.

Babies do, animals too.

Everything grows.

Everything grows and grows.

Sisters do, brothers too.

Everything grows.

 **Try It Out**

Make a class list of things that grow.

# Tell what you learned.

**1.** Look at the pictures. What happens when you grow and change?

2 years old

6 years old

**2.** Draw a picture. Show an animal you've seen grow. Tell how it changed.

**3.** Draw a picture to show how Little Gorilla looked at his birthday party. Tell what happened to Little Gorilla.

# At School

## Tell what you know.

How do children get to school?

# The Wheels on the Bus

The wheels on the bus go round and round
Round and round, round and round.
The wheels on the bus go round and round
All around the town.

**Talk About It**

How do you get
to school?

41

# Who do we see at school?

**Word Bank**

classroom

library

office

principal

children and teacher

Where are the children
and the teacher?

Where is the principal?

Where is the librarian?

Where is the nurse?

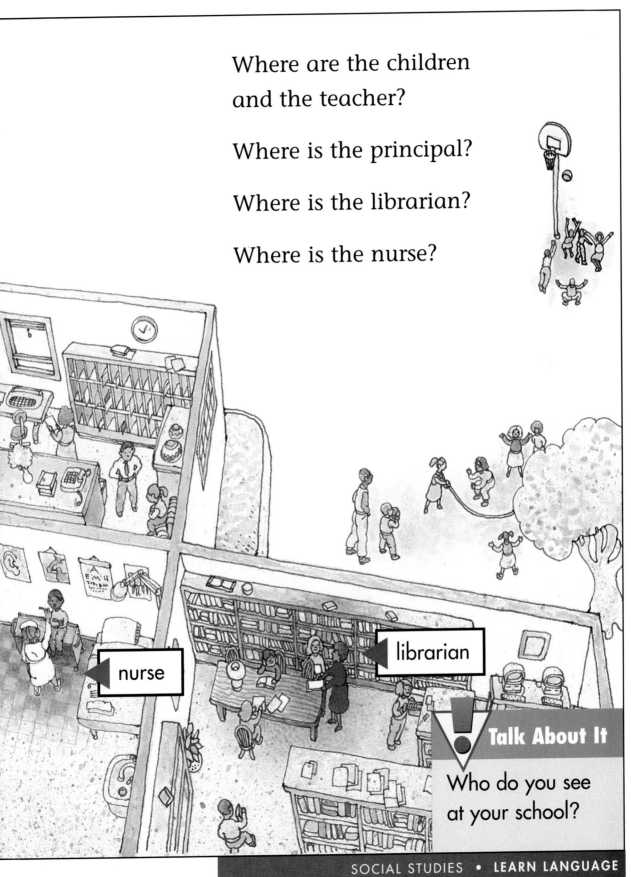

nurse

librarian

**Talk About It**

Who do you see
at your school?

# What do we do at school?

We listen.

We talk.

We read.

We think.

We draw.

We write.

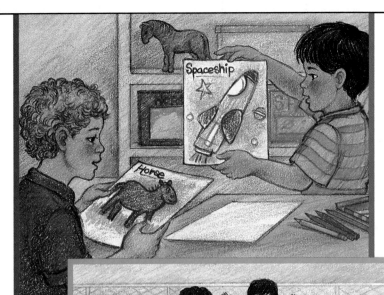

We share.

We play.

We take turns.

## We Chant.

When **do** we go to school?

Monday, Tuesday, Wednesday,

Thursday, and Friday too.

I think it's fun, don't you?

**Draw About It**

Draw something
you do at school.

# What are rules?

**Rules** tell us what to do.

Your school has rules.

Come to school on time.

Listen to your teacher.

Games have rules.

Take turns. ▶

Jump over the rope. ▶

**Think About It**

Why do we have rules?

# How many?

## Word Bank

1 one

2 two

3 three

4 four

5 five

6 six

7 seven

8 eight

9 nine

10 ten

How many children are listening?

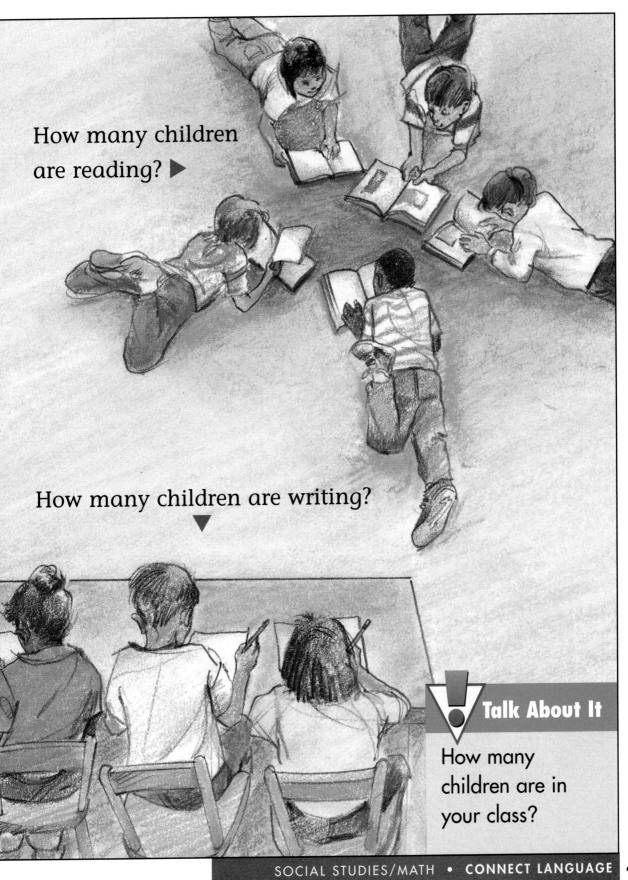

How many children
are reading? ▶

How many children are writing?
▼

**Talk About It**

How many
children are in
your class?

# My School, Your School

*by Bette Birnbaum*

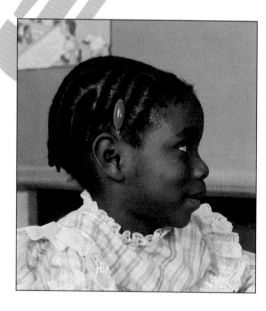

Here I am at my school. That's me at my
desk, saying good morning to my teacher.
My teacher's name is Mrs. Siegal.

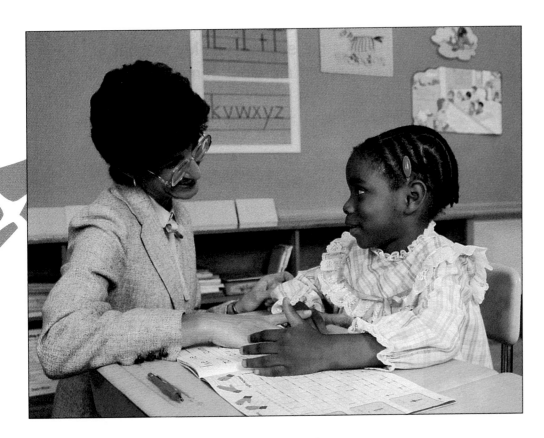

**What is your teacher's name?**

Here I am at my school. That's me saying "O." My teacher is playing an alphabet game with us.

**What games do you play in school?**

Here I am at my school. That's me and Billy with a shape puzzle. We like working together. We are best friends.

**Who are your friends at school?**

Here I am at my school. That's me writing a story at the computer. I like to write stories about dinosaurs.

**What do you like to write about?**

Here I am at my school. That's me in the middle circle. After lunch I like to play in the school yard with my friends.

**What do you like to do after lunch?**

Here I am at my school. That's me coloring in my math workbook. Math is what I like to do best at school.

**What do you like to do best at school?**

Here I am at my school. That's me playing the maracas. For music we usually sing songs, but today we are playing instruments.

**What does your class do for music?**

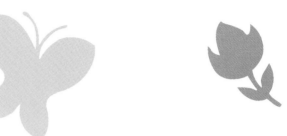

Here I am at my school. That's me in the wolf costume. Can you guess what play we are putting on? Putting on plays is one of the special things we do at school.

**What special things do you do at school?**

Here I am at my school. That's me reading a book to my friends. Sometimes we read at the end of the day.

**When do you read books in school?**

Here I am after school. That's me with
my friend Tasha at the bus stop across
the street from my house. My mom is
waiting for us. I can't wait to tell her all
about my day!

**What will you tell about your day?**

# The First Day of School

*by Sarah Wilson*

Hello, hello.
I'm new. Are you?
I'm shy, but I'm
excited, too.

I'm going to sing
and string a kite
and run and jump
and read and write

and talk about
the stars in space
and make new friends!
I like this place!

 **Try It Out**

Act out the poem
as you say it.

# Tell what you learned.

**1.** Name one rule you follow at your school.

**2.** Who do you see in the pictures? What are they doing?

**3.** Draw a picture. Show what you like best at school.

# Learning

## Tell what you know.

What do you **learn** in school?

# The Alphabet Song

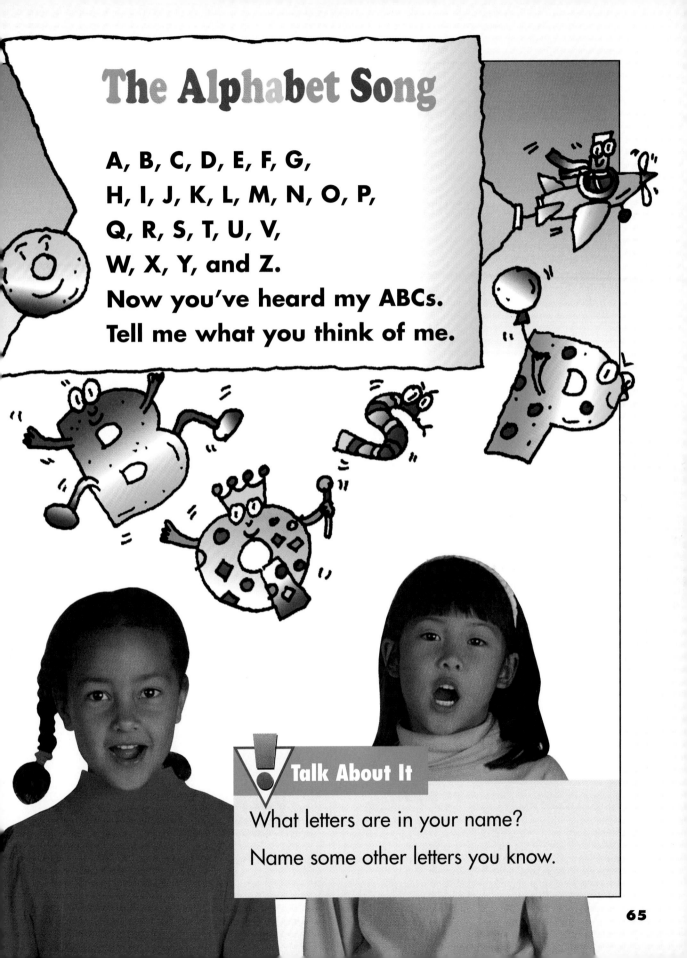

A, B, C, D, E, F, G,
H, I, J, K, L, M, N, O, P,
Q, R, S, T, U, V,
W, X, Y, and Z.
Now you've heard my ABCs.
Tell me what you think of me.

## Talk About It

What letters are in your name?

Name some other letters you know.

# What do we learn in school?

We learn to think.

We learn to ▶
read.

◀ We learn to
write.

We learn to ▶
**count.**

◀ We learn to read maps and globes.

We learn about ▶ people.

◀ We learn about other living things.

We learn from each other.

 **Talk About It**

What do you do at school?

# We practice in school.

**Practice** means to do something many times.

We learn how to do things by practicing them.

◀ We practice singing songs.

We practice playing ▶ games.

◀ We practice writing words.

We practice speaking words. ▶

◀ We practice acting out stories.

**Draw About It**

Draw something you practice at school.

# What can you do alone?

**Word Bank**

run

skip

walk

I can write.

I can read.

I can draw.

# What can you do in a group?

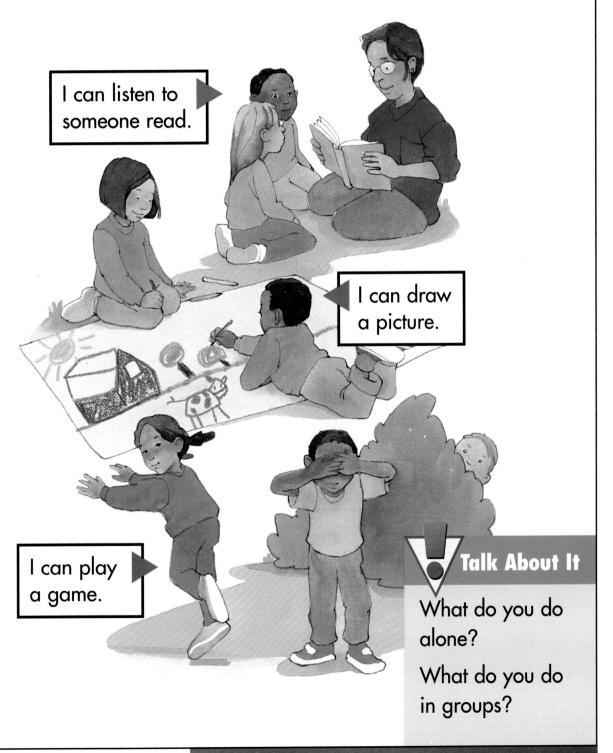

I can listen to someone read.

I can draw a picture.

I can play a game.

**Talk About It**

What do you do alone?

What do you do in groups?

# How do children feel at school?

Children have different **feelings** at different times.

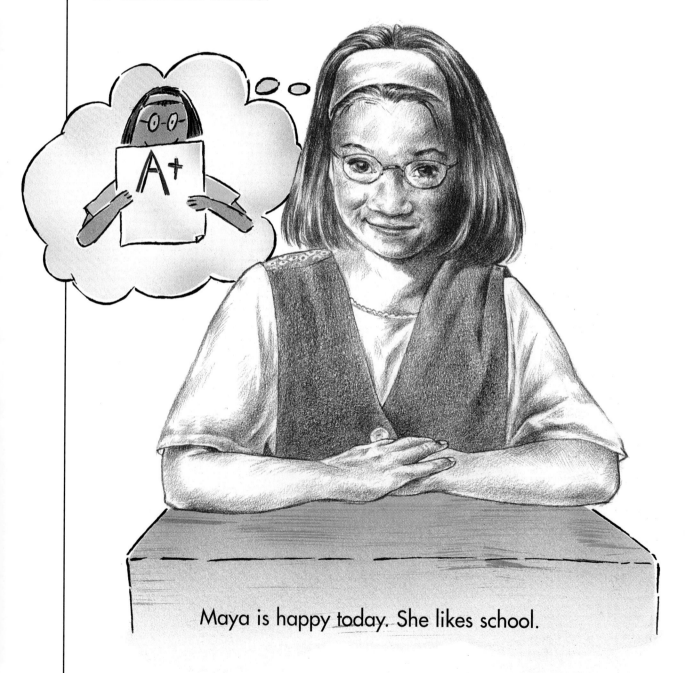

Maya is happy today. She likes school.

Samuel is sad today.
He misses his friend.

Paul is scared today.
He is a new student.

**Think About It**

How can you help
a new student
who is scared?

# I Like School

Mayeline Bonilla
age 7

I like school because it's fun. We do fun things like art and gym. We also go to the park.

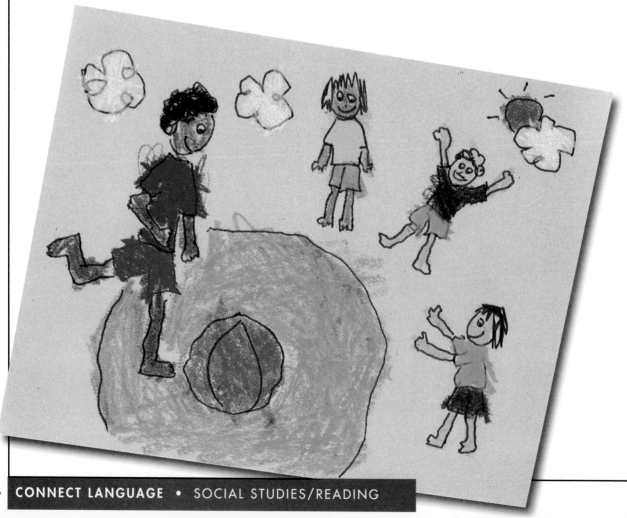

In my class, we put together a city.
I made a house.

I like to do fun things in my
classroom. I like to do fun things
with my teacher.

# If You're Happy
## and You Know It

If you're happy and you know it,
clap your hands (**clap, clap**).

If you're happy and you know it,
clap your hands (**clap, clap**).

If you're happy and you know it,
then your face will surely show it.

If you're happy and you know it,
clap your hands (**clap, clap**).

**Try It Out**

Think of other verses to the song.

Sing them together.

# Tell what you learned.

**1.** Name something you learn in school. How are you learning it?

**2.** What are the children doing? Are they alone or in a group?

**3.** Draw a picture. Show something fun to do in a group. Tell about your picture.

# Tell what you know.

Where do people live?

# Neighbors

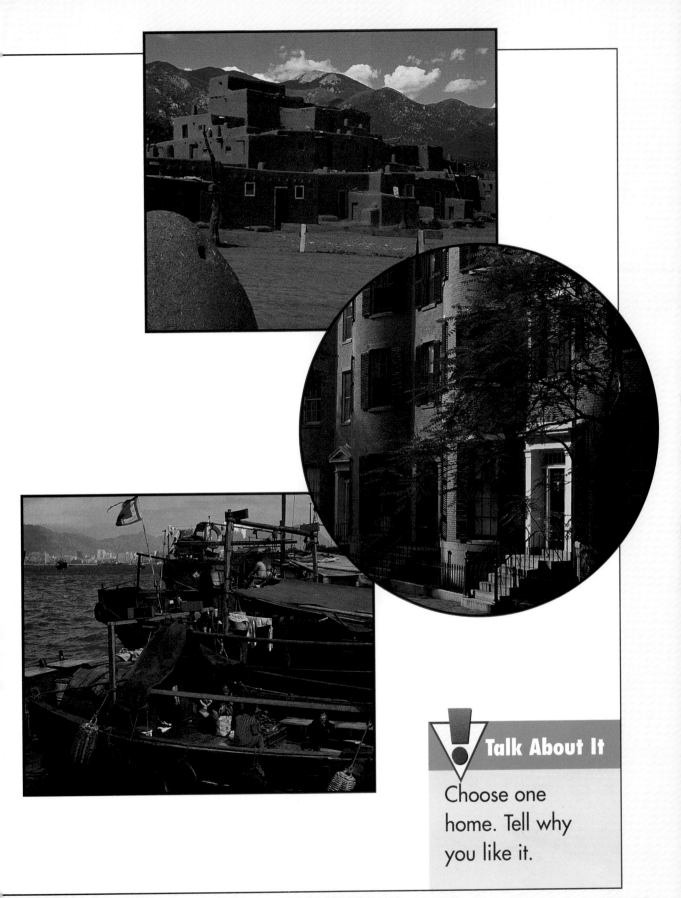

**Talk About It**

Choose one
home. Tell why
you like it.

# What is a neighborhood?

A **neighborhood** is a place where families live near each other.

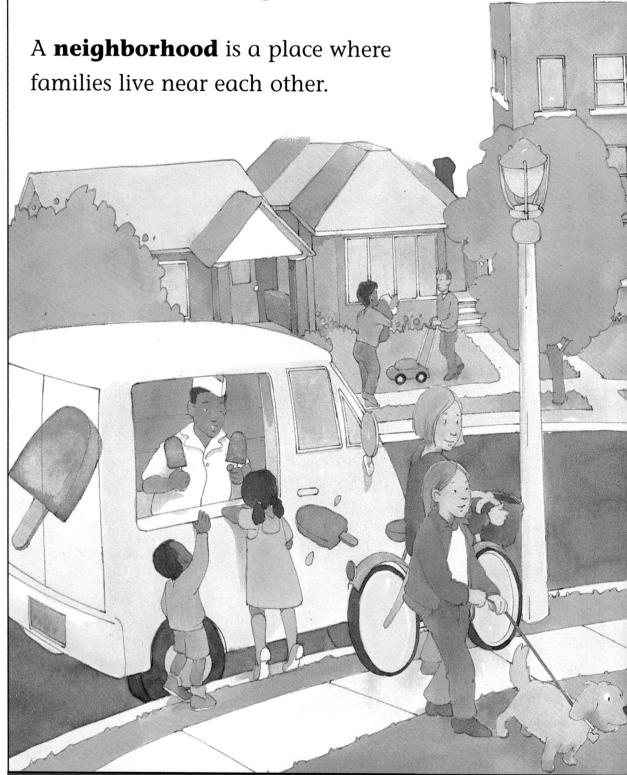

# What are neighbors?

**Neighbors** are people who live near each other.

Neighbors help each other.

Neighbors can play together too.

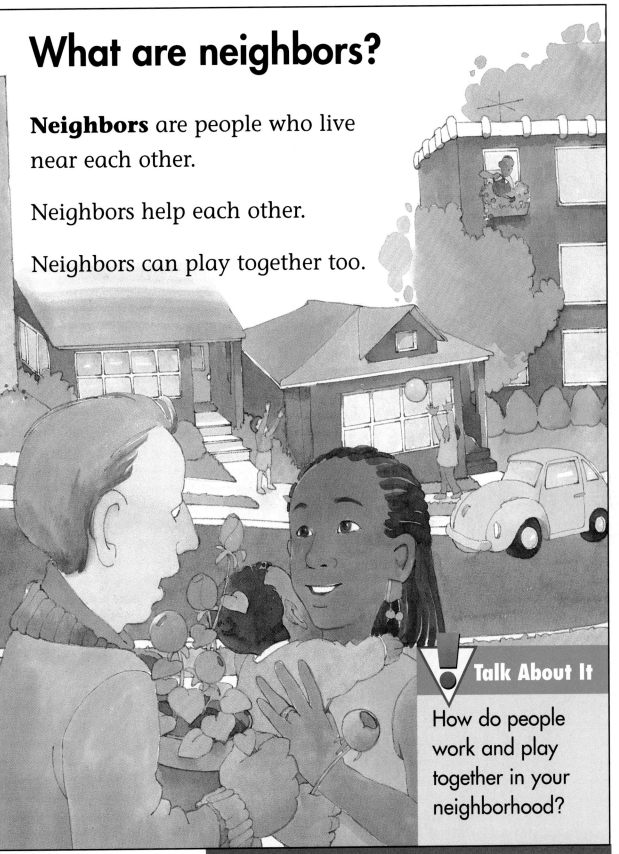

## Talk About It

How do people work and play together in your neighborhood?

# How do maps help us?

**Maps** show us where to find places.

A neighborhood map shows streets and houses.

**Talk About It**

Tell what you see in this neighborhood.

# What is a community?

A **community** is bigger than a neighborhood.

A community is where groups of people live and work.

A community has houses, apartments, and other places.

PINE

OAK

fire station

Find the library on the map.

Find the park on the map.

What else do you see?

Word Bank

**go**

**stop**

**turn**

**left**

**right**

**go straight**

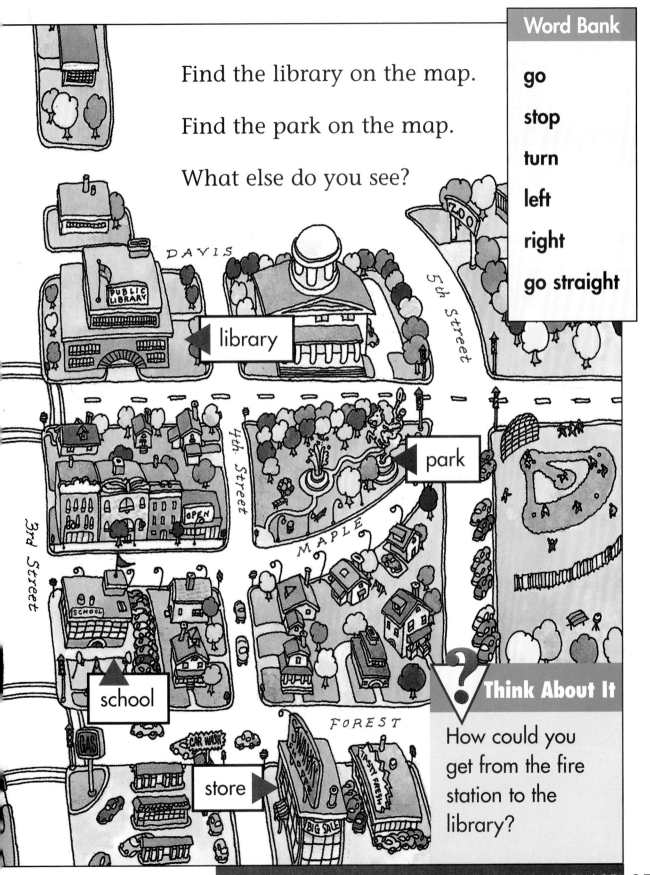

DAVIS

PUBLIC LIBRARY

5th Street

library

4th Street

park

3rd Street

MAPLE

OPEN

SCHOOL

school

GAS

FOREST

CAR WASH

store

BIG SALE

ZOO

**? Think About It**

How could you get from the fire station to the library?

# What animals live in a park?

Squirrels can live in a park.

Ducks can live in a park.

pigeons ▶

ducks ▶

How many ducks are in this picture?

How many squirrels are in this picture?

robin ▶

chipmunks ▼

squirrels ▲

**Draw About It**

Draw a picture of animals that live in a park near you.

# One Afternoon

*by Yumi Heo*

Minho liked to do errands with his mother.

One afternoon, they went to the Laundromat
to drop off their clothes and then to the
beauty salon to get his mother's hair cut.

At the ice cream store, Minho got a vanilla cone.

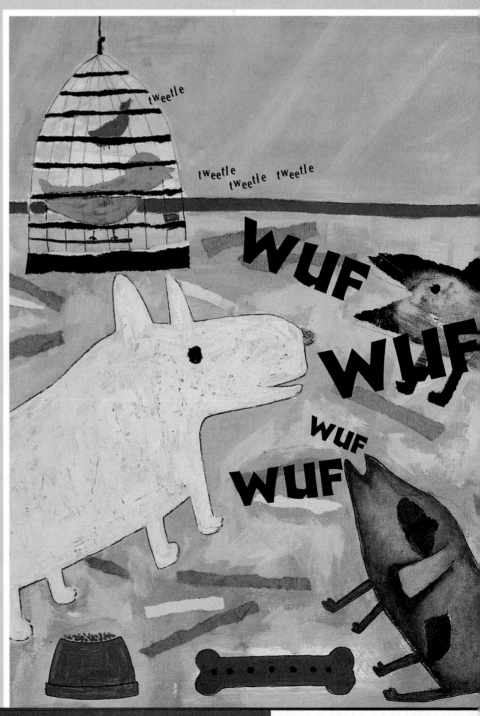

They looked in the pet store window at
the puppies, kittens, hamsters, and birds.

They picked up his father's shoes at the shoe repair store and got food for dinner at the supermarket.

Last of all, Minho and his mother went
back to the Laundromat to get the clothes
they had dropped off.

Traffic was very heavy on the street because of the construction.

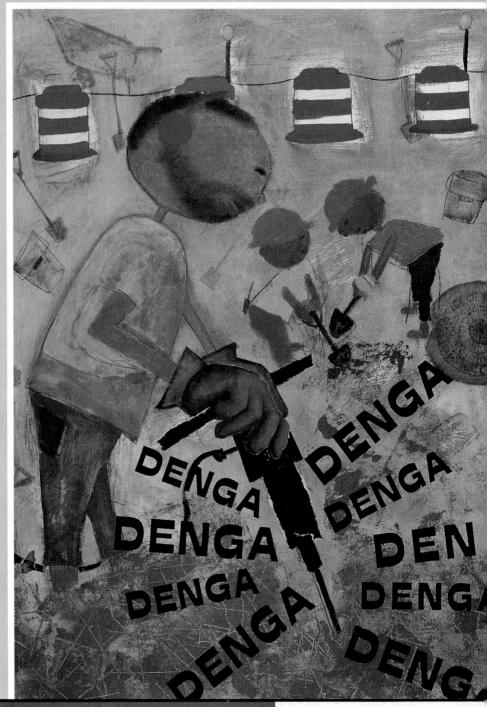

A fire engine tried to get through.

The El train was passing by above.

Near Minho's apartment, children were playing stickball.

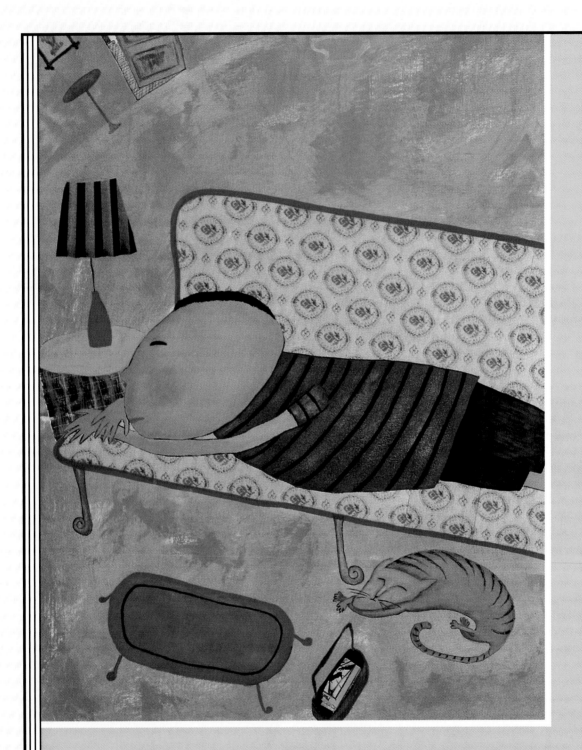

Minho and his mother were very happy
to be back in their quiet home. Minho
was tired and fell asleep on the couch.

But from the bathroom . . .

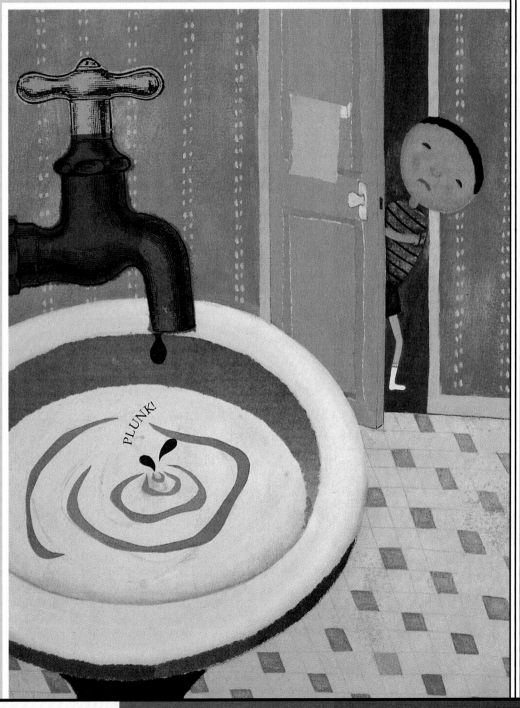

# My Street

### words and music by Malvina Reynolds

My street is a friendly street,
People say hello to the people they meet,
People walk along with the happy feet
On my street, Yes.
Little kids, big kids, the women and men,
Know you by your name and they knew you when,
Know where you're going and where you've been,
On my street, Yes!

HOLA    CIAO    SHALOM    CHÀO EM

### Try It Out

Say **hello** in two languages.

# Tell what you learned.

**1.** What do neighbors do together?

**2.** Look at the map. What is near the school?

**3.** Name a place Minho and his mother went.

# Animals and Their Homes

# Tell what you know.

Where can animals live?

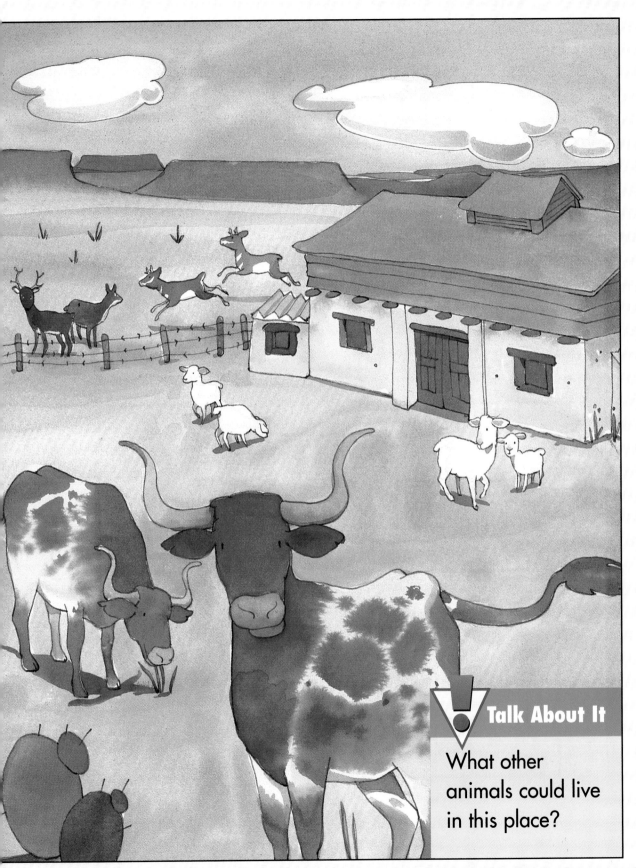

**Talk About It**

What other animals could live in this place?

# What animals do you see?

Name the animals.

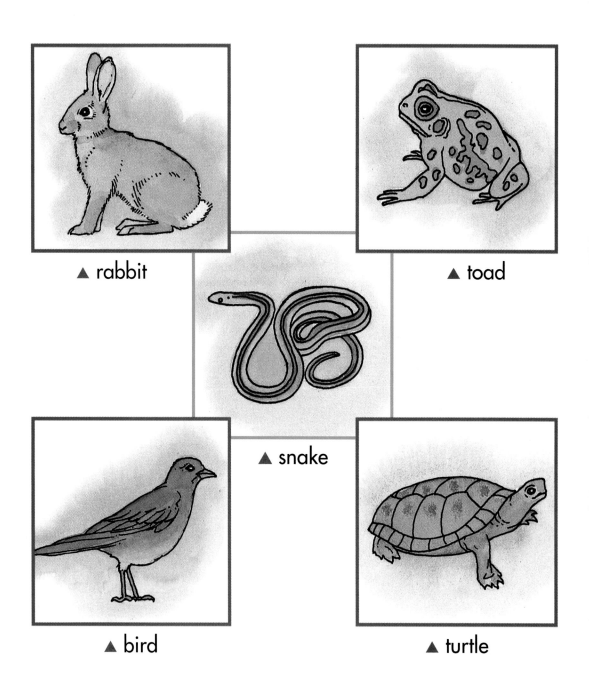

▲ rabbit

▲ toad

▲ snake

▲ bird

▲ turtle

# Where do these animals live?

Which animals live in a pond?

Which animals live in a field?

Which animals live in a tree?

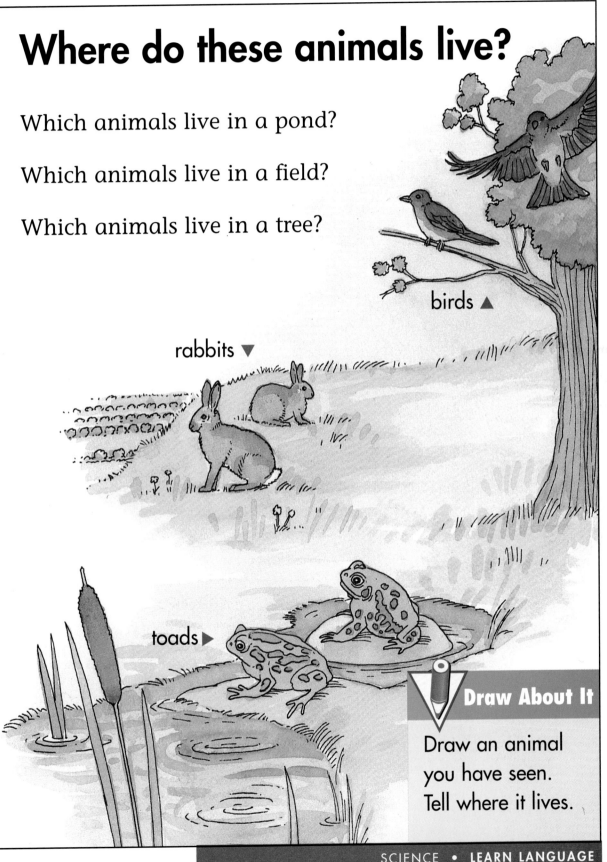

birds ▲

rabbits ▼

toads ▶

**Draw About It**

Draw an animal you have seen. Tell where it lives.

# What animals live at a zoo?

The seal swims in water.

The monkey climbs in trees.

◀ seal

monkey ▶

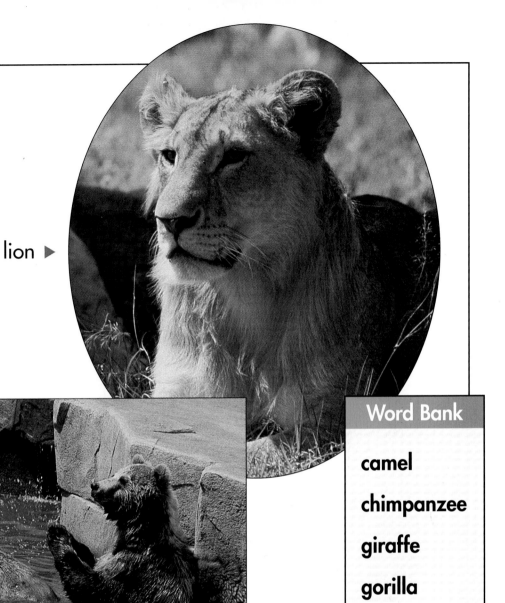

lion ▶

bears ▼

**Word Bank**

camel

chimpanzee

giraffe

gorilla

tiger

The lion rests in tall grass.

The bears play on rocks.

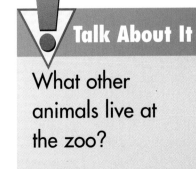

**Talk About It**

What other animals live at the zoo?

# How do animals use trees for homes?

Some animals live on the branches of a tree.

Some animals live in holes in a tree.

Some animals live on the leaves of a tree.

caterpillar ▼

squirrel ▶

raccoon ▶

Birds build nests in trees.

This bird builds a big nest.

This bird builds a small nest.

This bird builds a nest that looks like a basket.

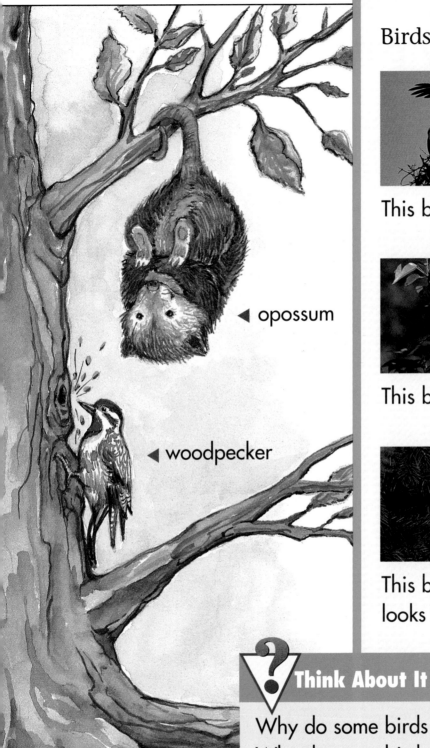

◄ opossum

◄ woodpecker

## Think About It

Why do some birds build big nests?
Why do some birds build small nests?

# How many pets?

Some people keep animals as pets.

Laura has one mouse and one turtle.
How many pets does she have in all?

Marcus has one dog.
The dog has three puppies.
How many pets does Marcus have in all?

Olivia has four kittens.
She gave one to Bobby.
How many kittens does Olivia have left?

**Talk About It**

Tell about a pet you would like to have. Tell where your pet might live.

# Taking Care of Pets

Pets need their owners to care
for them.
They need food, water, exercise,
and a place to sleep.

How will the boy take care of his puppy?

The boy will *give food to* his puppy.

The boy will *give water to* his puppy.

The boy will take his puppy out for exercise.

The boy will make a cozy bed for his puppy.

**Talk About It**

How would you care for a puppy?

# The Furry Home

by J. M. Westrup

*If I were a mouse*
*And wanted a house*
*I think I would choose*
*My new red shoes.*
*Furry edges,*
*Fur inside,*
*What a lovely*
*Place to hide!*
*I'd not travel,*
*I'd not roam—*
*Just sit in*
*My furry home.*

## Try It Out

Pretend you are
a mouse.
Draw your house.

# Tell what you learned.

**1.** Name two places animals can live.

**2.** Make a web like this one. Add the names of animals that live in each place.

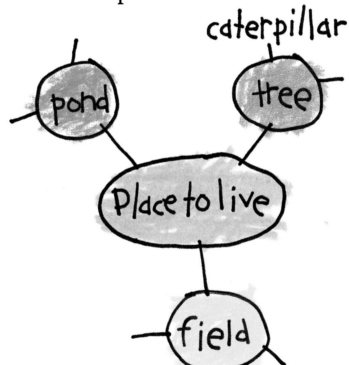

**3.** A pet needs water. What else does a pet need?

# How You Can Feel Safe

# Tell what you know.

Where is **safety** important?

▲ street

▲ car

▲ playground

▲ bus

soccer field ▲

beach ▶

**Talk About It**

Name other places where safety is important.

# Who helps keep you safe?

▲
Teachers
keep us safe
at school.

▲
Park rangers
keep us safe in
the park.

▲
Coaches keep
us safe on the
ball field.

Our families keep us safe at home.

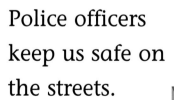

Police officers keep us safe on the streets.

**baby-sitter**

**crossing guard**

**firefighters**

## Think About It

Name other people who keep you safe.
What do they do?

# How can you cross the street safely?

Obey the traffic lights.

Wait for the green light.

Walk in the **crosswalk.**

Cross at the corner.

Look both ways.

Wait for **traffic** to pass.

## Draw About It

Draw a traffic light that shows go.

Draw a traffic light that shows stop.

# How can you stay safe in a car?

Always use a seat belt.

Always keep your head and arms
in the car.

Don't bother the driver.

# How can you stay safe on the playground?

Take turns.

Do not push.

Keep out of the way of others.

Do not talk to strangers.

**Talk About It**

Tell how you keep safe.

# What are germs?

**Germs** are very small.

You cannot see them.

Some germs make you sick.

You can wash germs away.

# When can a doctor help you?

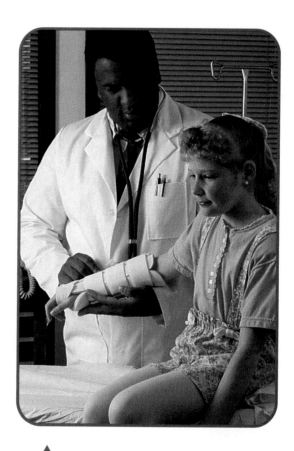

▲

A **doctor** can help you when you are sick.

▲

A doctor can help you when you are hurt.

## Talk About It

Tell about a time a doctor helped you.

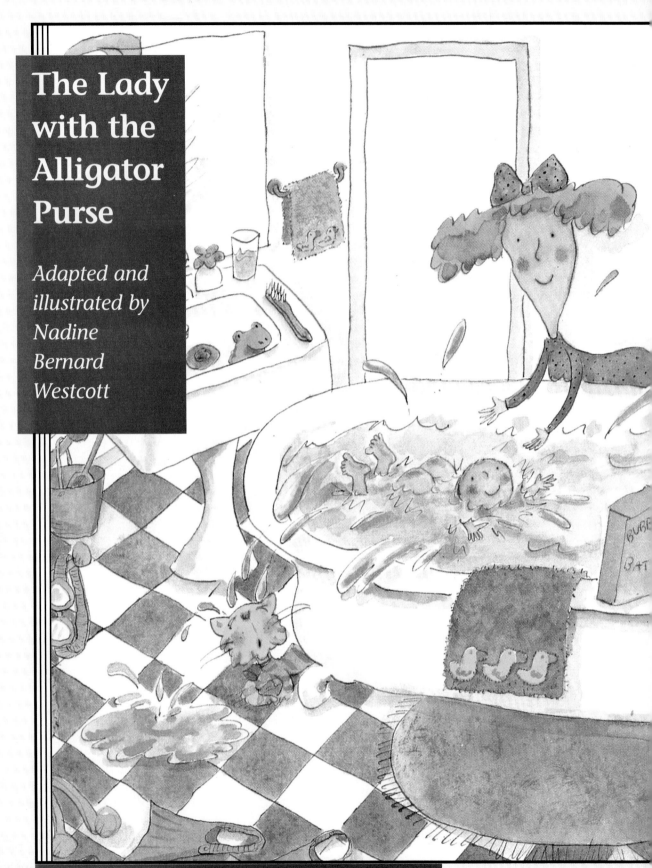

# The Lady with the Alligator Purse

*Adapted and illustrated by Nadine Bernard Westcott*

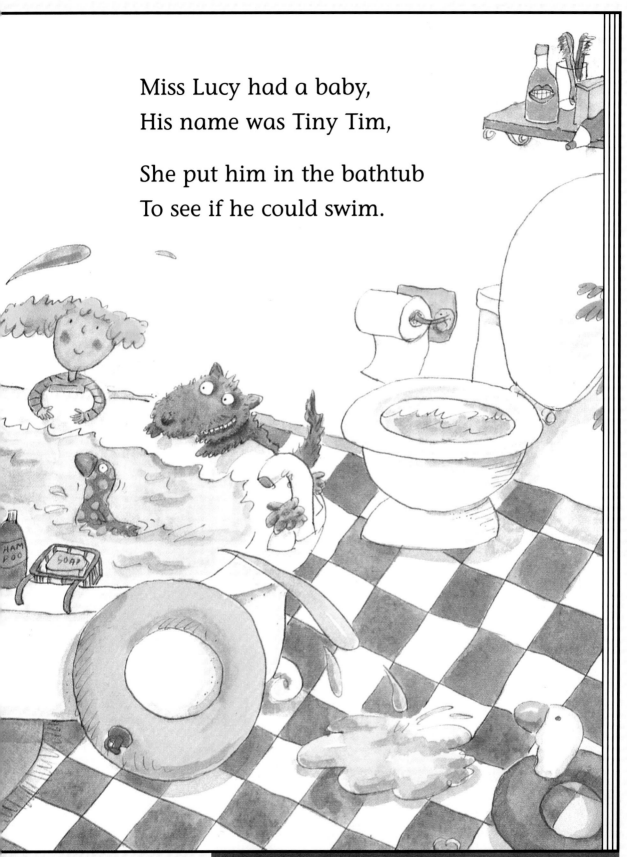

Miss Lucy had a baby,
His name was Tiny Tim,

She put him in the bathtub
To see if he could swim.

He drank up all the water,
He ate up all the soap,

He tried to eat the bathtub,
But it wouldn't go down his throat.

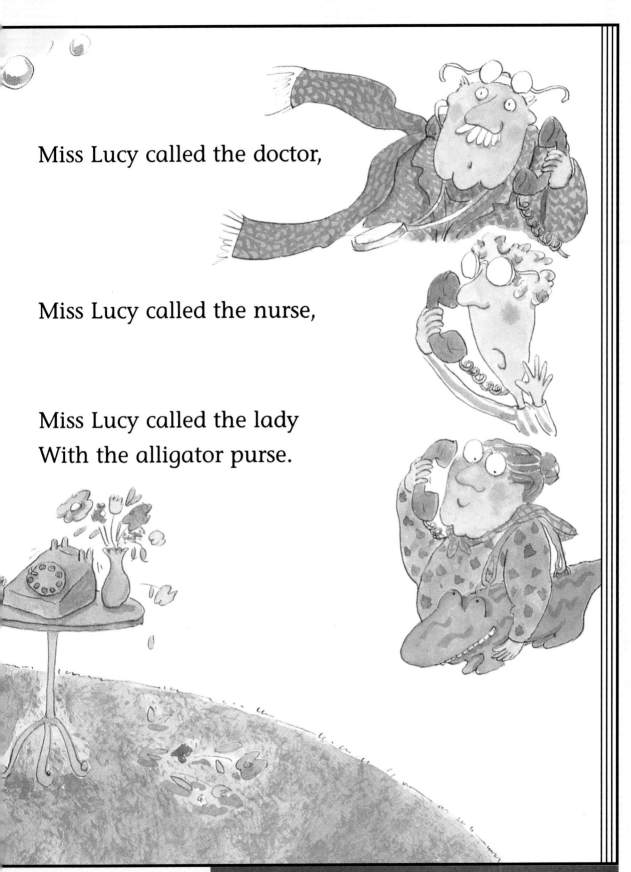

Miss Lucy called the doctor,

Miss Lucy called the nurse,

Miss Lucy called the lady
With the alligator purse.

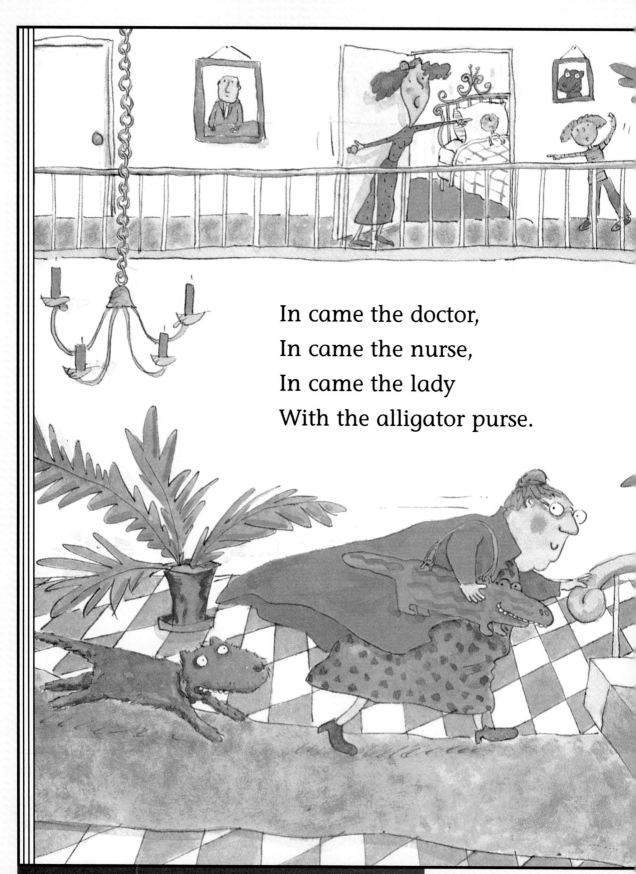

In came the doctor,
In came the nurse,
In came the lady
With the alligator purse.

"Mumps," said the doctor,
"Measles," said the nurse,

"Nonsense!" said the lady
With the alligator purse.

"Penicillin," said the doctor,
"Castor oil," said the nurse,

"Pizza!" said the lady
With the alligator purse.

Out went the doctor,
Out went the nurse,

Out went the lady
With the alligator purse.

# Look Both Ways

by Dee Lillegard

I never run across the street—
I always stop to see
If something big is coming in
The direction of *me*.

You never know—
There might be cars.
There also might be
DINOSAURS!

And what if one
Should step on me!
That's why I always
Stop to see.

**Try It Out**

Name an action for friends to do.
Say "Green Light" to start.
Say "Red Light" to stop.

# Tell what you learned.

**1.** Name some workers who help keep you safe.

**2.** Tell what you do before you cross a street.

**3.** Draw a picture to show the three people Miss Lucy called to help Tiny Tim.

# How You Can Feel Healthy

## Tell what you know.

What are they doing?

Why are these things good to do?

## Word Bank

**drink**

**sleep**

**wash**

## Talk About It

What do you do
to feel healthy?

# Why is it good to exercise?

How do they get **exercise?**

How does this help them?

## Word Bank

**bike**

**hike**

**skate**

**skip**

**swim**

There are other ways to exercise too.

Work with a partner.
Make a list.
Share it with the class.

## Talk About It

How do you like
to exercise?

# Keeping Healthy

Ask a partner.

What are they doing to keep **healthy?**

How does this help?

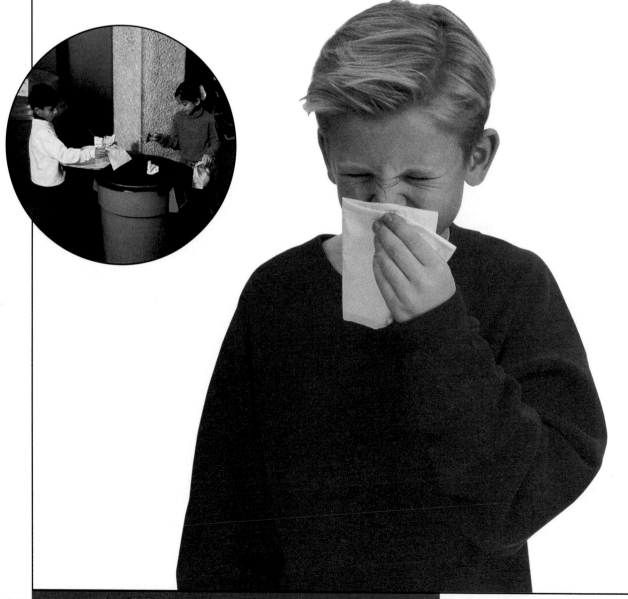

# How do you keep clean and healthy?

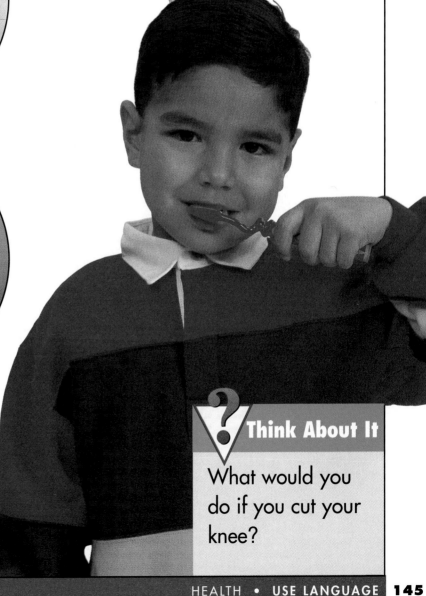

Make a class list.

Tell what you do.

**? Think About It**

What would you do if you cut your knee?

# What kinds of foods help you grow and be healthy?

You need some of these foods each day.

What kinds of foods do you need most?

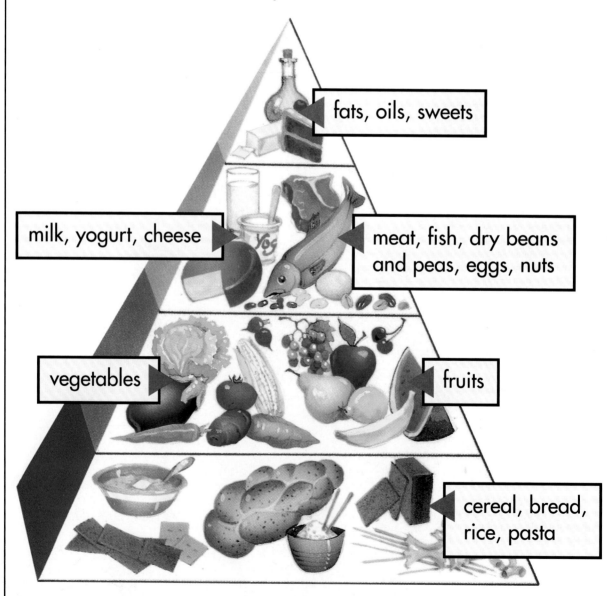

fats, oils, sweets

milk, yogurt, cheese

meat, fish, dry beans and peas, eggs, nuts

vegetables

fruits

cereal, bread, rice, pasta

# Make a food chart.

**1.** Draw **vegetables** on one side.

**2.** Draw **fruits** on the other side.

## Word Bank

**beans**

**grapes**

**oranges**

**peas**

**potatoes**

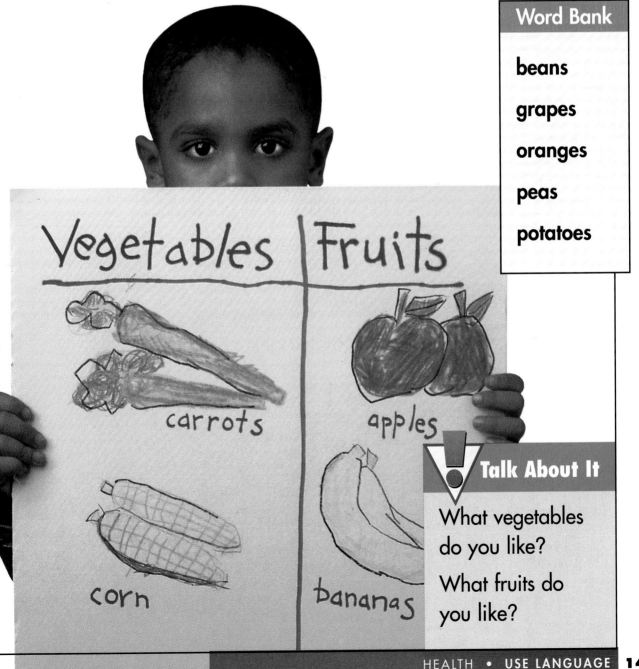

Vegetables | Fruits

carrots

apples

corn

bananas

## Talk About It

What vegetables do you like?

What fruits do you like?

# How many in all?

| Maria's Chart | |
|---|---|
| Monday | 🥕 |
| Tuesday | 🥕🥕 |
| Wednesday | 🥕🥕 |
| Thursday | 🥕🥕🥕 |
| Friday | 🥕🥕 |

How many carrots did Maria
eat in all?

| Shu's Chart | |
|---|---|
| Monday | 🍲 |
| Tuesday | 🍲🍲 |
| Wednesday | 🍲 |
| Thursday | 🍲 |
| Friday | 🍲🍲 |

How many bowls of soup did
Shu eat in all?

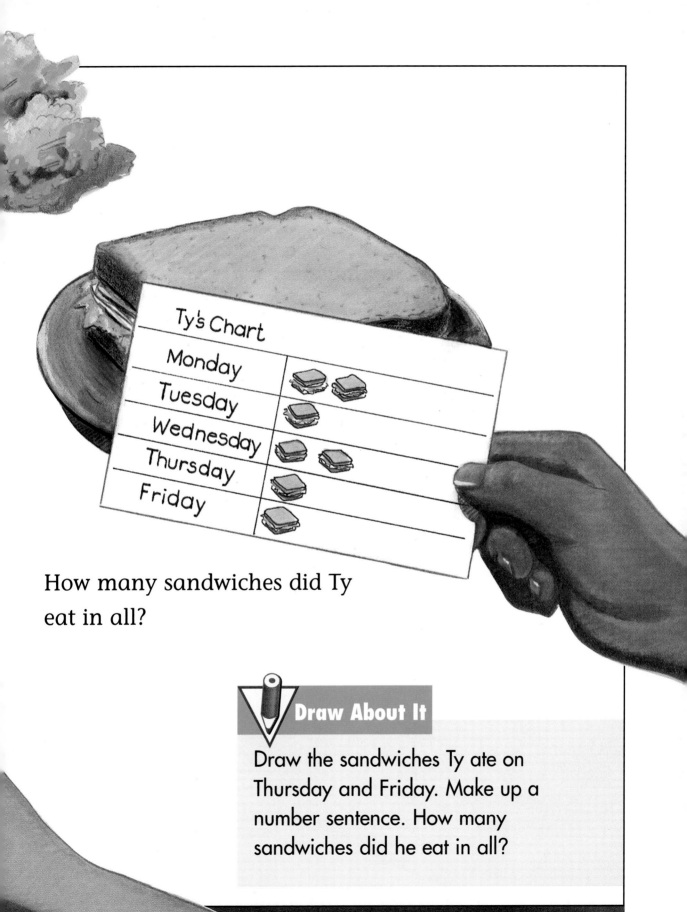

| Ty's Chart | |
| --- | --- |
| Monday | |
| Tuesday | |
| Wednesday | |
| Thursday | |
| Friday | |

How many sandwiches did Ty eat in all?

## Draw About It

Draw the sandwiches Ty ate on Thursday and Friday. Make up a number sentence. How many sandwiches did he eat in all?

# Allie Alligator

by Babs Bell Hajdusiewicz

When all the other alligators
    went off for a swim,
Little Allie Alligator
    went into the gym.

She saw giraffes play basketball.
   She saw the foxes run.
She saw gorillas climb the ropes
   and then when they were done . . .

Allie tried to climb the ropes.
   She tried to throw the ball.
She tried to run around the track,
   but alligators crawl!

So Allie ran to get her suit
and crawled into the pool.
"I'm glad I'm long and flat," she said.
"And swimming makes me cool."

## Try It Out

Act out an exercise you like to do. Ask classmates to guess what exercise you are doing.

# Tell what you learned.

**1.** What do you do to stay healthy?

**2.** Name some foods that help you grow and stay healthy.

**3.** What was Allie good at? How did Allie feel at the end of the story?

# Using Our Senses

## Tell what you know.

What can you see?

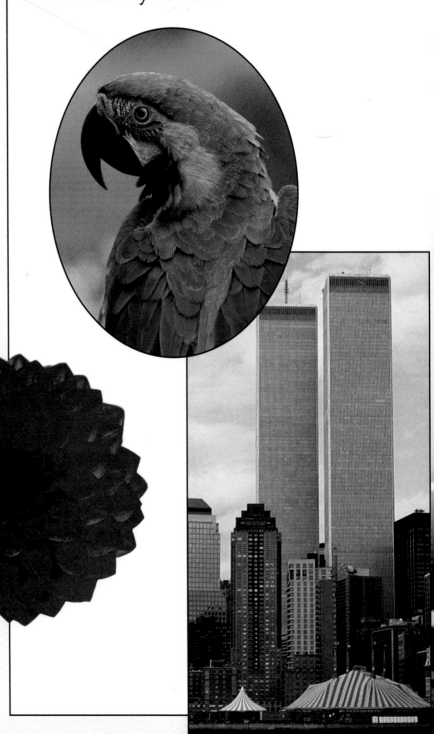

# What can you hear?

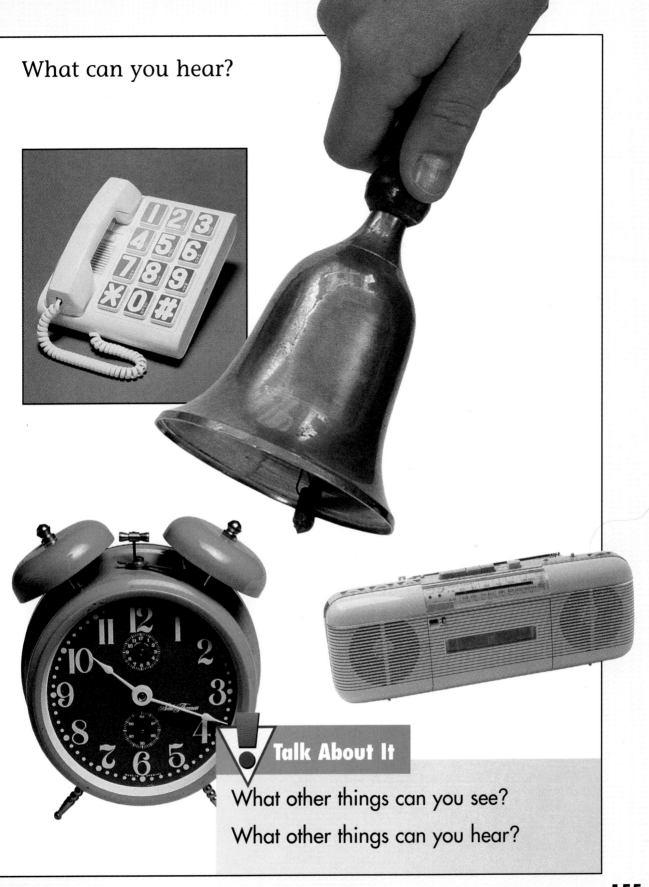

## Talk About It

What other things can you see?

What other things can you hear?

155

# Senses and Body Parts

What's happening in the park?

She sees a butterfly.

She hears a bird.

He feels the water.

She smells flowers.

Make a class chart.
Tell which part of the
body is used.

| Sense | Body Part |
|-------|-----------|
| hear  |           |
| see   |           |
| taste |           |
| smell |           |
| touch |           |

He tastes an apple.

eye ——————
nose ——————
tongue ——————

ear

hand

**Talk About It**

You are in the
park. What else
can you see, hear,
touch, or taste?

# What can your senses tell you?

ball        bird

You see colors and shapes.

What is round?
What is red?

kitten      lion

You hear sounds.

What is loud?
What is soft?

skunk          flower

You smell things.

What smells good?
What smells bad?

lemon          pretzel

You taste things.

What tastes sour?
What tastes salty?

rock          yo-yo

You touch things.

What feels smooth?
What feels bumpy?

**Draw About It**

Draw something
you like to taste.

# How can you take care of your eyes and ears?

Wear sunglasses on sunny days.

Never look right at the sun.

Cover your ears when you're near loud sounds.

Turn down loud music.

How do these workers take care of their eyes and ears?

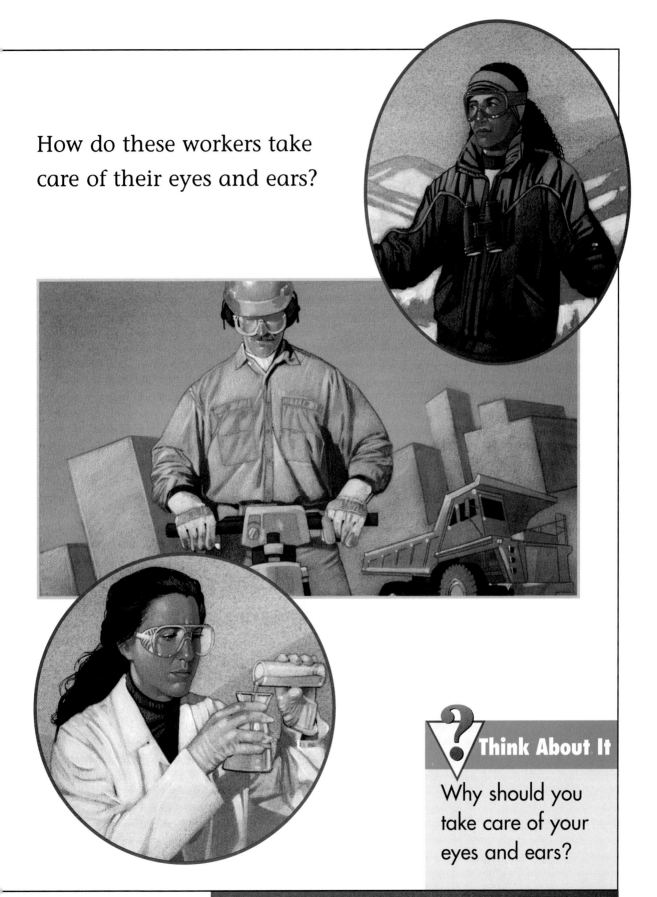

**Think About It**

Why should you take care of your eyes and ears?

# Make high and low sounds.

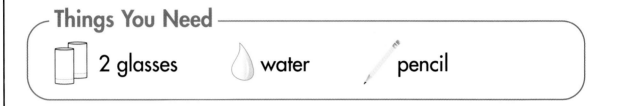

2 glasses     water     pencil

## Follow these steps.

**1.** Fill the first glass almost to the top.

**2.** Fill the second glass halfway.

**3.** Tap each glass with the pencil.

**4.** Which sounds higher?

My Record

The first glass
sounds _____.

The second glass
sounds _____.

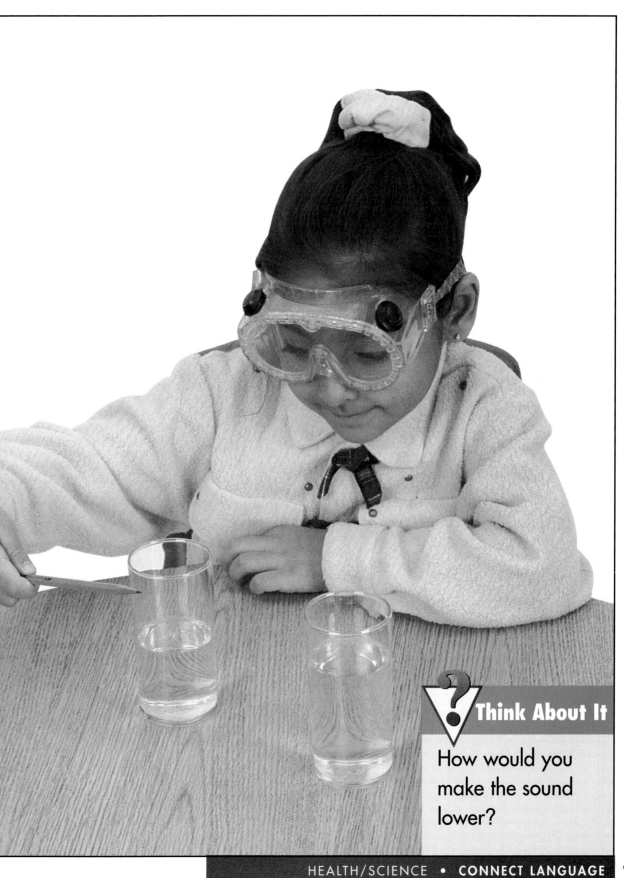

## Think About It

How would you make the sound lower?

# Peace at Last

*by Jill Murphy*

The hour was late.
Mr. Bear was tired,
Mrs. Bear was tired,
and Baby Bear was tired,
so they all went to bed.
Mrs. Bear fell asleep.
Mr. Bear didn't.
Mrs. Bear began to snore.

"SNORE," went Mrs. Bear.
"SNORE, SNORE, SNORE."
"Oh, NO!" said Mr. Bear,
"I can't stand THIS."
So he got up and went to
sleep in Baby Bear's room.

Baby Bear was not asleep either.
He was lying in bed, pretending
to be an airplane.
"NYAAOW!" went Baby Bear.
"NYAAOW! NYAAOW!"
"Oh, NO!" said Mr. Bear,
"I can't stand THIS."
So he got up
and went to sleep in the living room.

TICK-TOCK...went the living room
clock....TICK-TOCK, TICK-TOCK,
CUCKOO! CUCKOO!
"Oh, NO!" said Mr. Bear,
"I can't stand THIS."
So he went off to sleep in the kitchen.

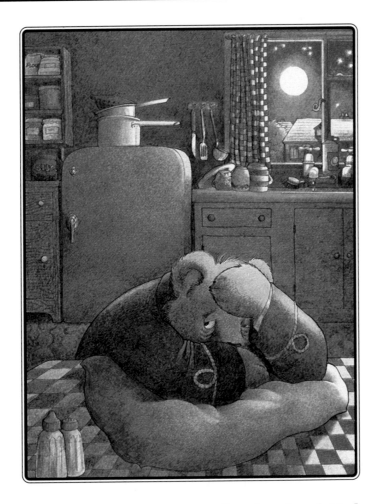

DRIP, DRIP…went the leaky kitchen
faucet.
HMMMMMMMMMM…
went the refrigerator.
"Oh, NO!" said Mr. Bear,
"I can't stand THIS."
So he got up
and went to sleep in the garden.

Well, you would not believe
what noises there are in
the garden at night.
"TOO-WHIT-TOO-WHOO!"
went the owl.
"SNUFFLE, SNUFFLE," went
the hedgehog.
"MIAAAOW!" sang the cats
on the wall.
"Oh, NO!" said Mr. Bear,
"I can't stand THIS."
So he went off to sleep in
the car.

It was cold in the car
and uncomfortable, but
Mr. Bear was so tired
that he didn't notice.
He was just falling asleep
when all the birds started to
sing and the sun peeped in at
the window.
"TWEET TWEET!" went the birds.
SHINE, SHINE…went the sun.
"Oh, NO!" said Mr. Bear,
"I can't stand THIS."
So he got up and went back
into the house.

In the house Baby Bear was fast asleep, and Mrs. Bear had turned over and wasn't snoring anymore.

Mr. Bear got into bed and closed his eyes.

"Peace at last," he said to himself.

BRRRRRRRRRRRRRR...went the alarm clock. BRRRRRR!

Mrs. Bear sat up and rubbed her eyes.

"Good morning, dear," she said.

"Did you sleep well?"

"Not VERY well, dear," yawned Mr. Bear.

"Never mind," said Mrs. Bear.

"I'll bring you the mail and a nice
cup of tea."

And she did.

# The Bear Went Over the Mountain

Oh, the bear went over the mountain,
The bear went over the mountain,
The bear went over the mountain
To see what he could see.

To see what he could see,
To see what he could see,

Oh, the bear went over the mountain,
The bear went over the mountain,
The bear went over the mountain
To see what he could see.

## Try It Out

Think of something the bear might see.
Give clues to help classmates guess
what you are thinking of.

# Tell what you learned.

**1.** Make a chart. Tell what each body part helps you do.

| Part of My Body | Helps Me |
|---|---|
| eyes | see |
| ears | |
| nose | |
| tongue | |
| hands | |

**2.** How can you take care of your eyes?

**3.** Why couldn't Mr. Bear sleep?

# How We See and Hear

## Tell what you know.

Look at the red line and the blue line.
Which is longer?
Which is shorter?

Look at the two lines.
Which is longer?
Which is shorter?

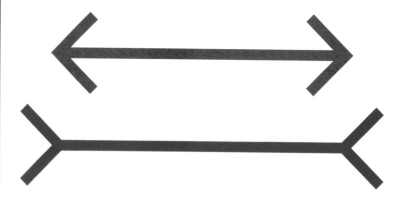

Use your ruler. Check your guess.

# Which makes a louder sound?

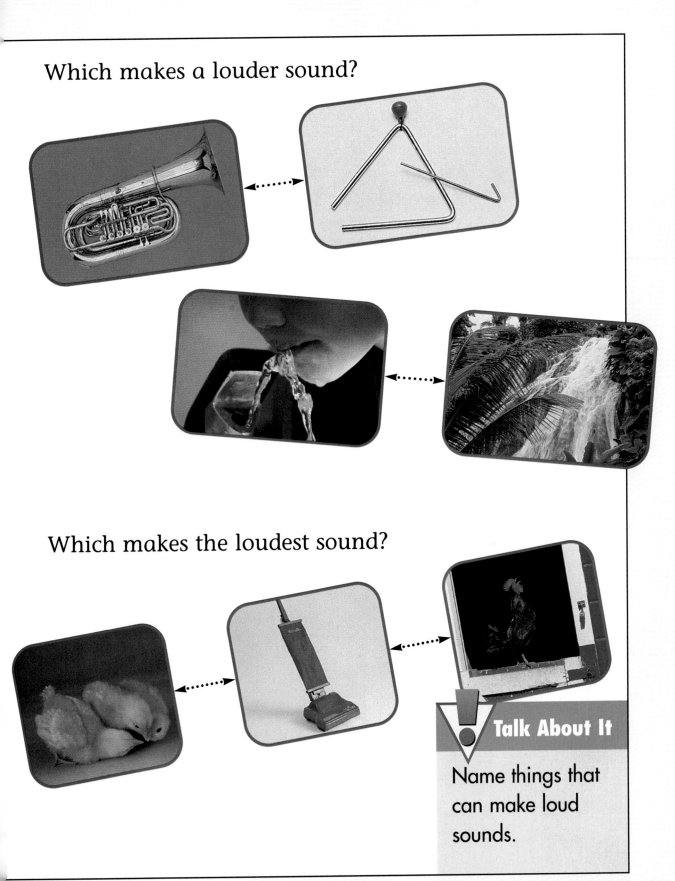

# Which makes the loudest sound?

## Talk About It

Name things that can make loud sounds.

# How do people and animals see?

People use their eyes to see.
Animals use their eyes too.

Some animals see very well at night.
When do people see best?

People have two eyes.

Most animals have two eyes.
But spiders have eight eyes.

▲ cat

▲ eagle

▲ rabbit

▲ spider

**Think About It**

What things do people use to help them see better?

# How do people and animals hear?

People use their ears to hear.
Most animals use their ears to hear too.
Some animals hear very well.

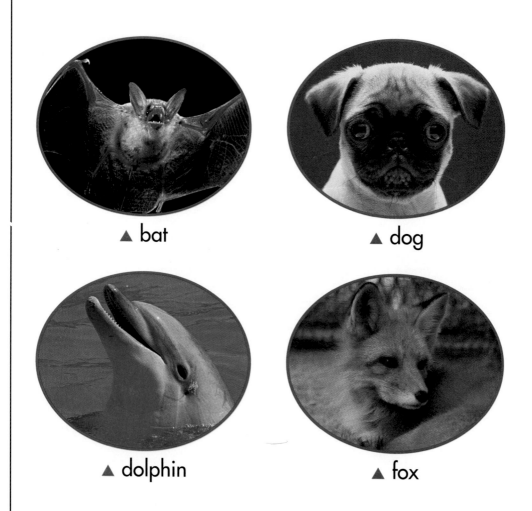

▲ bat

▲ dog

▲ dolphin

▲ fox

Some animals have very big ears.

Some animals' ears cannot be seen.

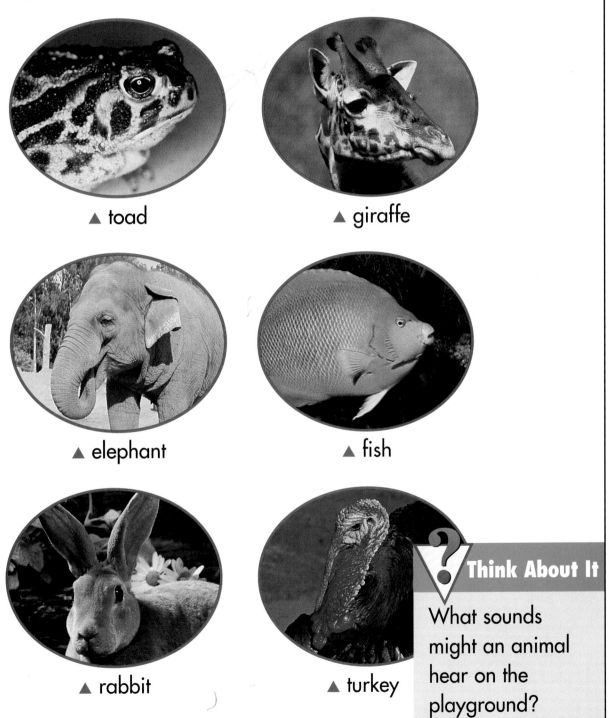

▲ toad

▲ giraffe

▲ elephant

▲ fish

▲ rabbit

▲ turkey

**Think About It**

What sounds might an animal hear on the playground?

# Do you see better with two eyes?

Let's find out.

**Things You Need**

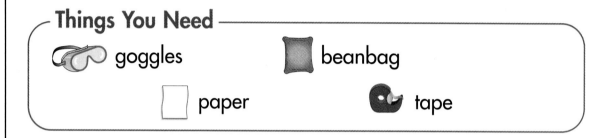

goggles

beanbag

paper

tape

## Follow these steps.

**1.** Have a partner toss a beanbag to you 10 times.

**2.** Count the times you catch it.

**3.** Tape paper over one side of the goggles.

**4.** Put the goggles on.

**5.** Have a partner toss the beanbag to you 10 times.

**6.** Count the times you catch it.

| | number of times beanbag was caught |
|---|---|
| using 1 eye | |
| using 2 eyes | |

**Write About It**

Make a chart like this one. Write how many times you caught the beanbag.

# How many things do you see?

Look at the picture.

How many police cars do you see?

How many green cars do you see?

How many fire engines do you see?

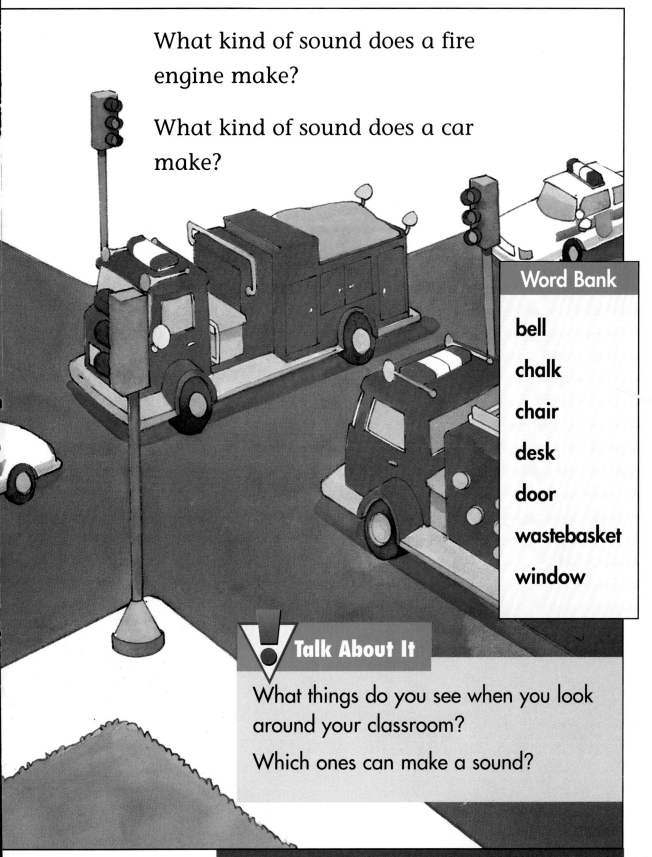

What kind of sound does a fire engine make?

What kind of sound does a car make?

## Word Bank

bell

chalk

chair

desk

door

wastebasket

window

## Talk About It

What things do you see when you look around your classroom?

Which ones can make a sound?

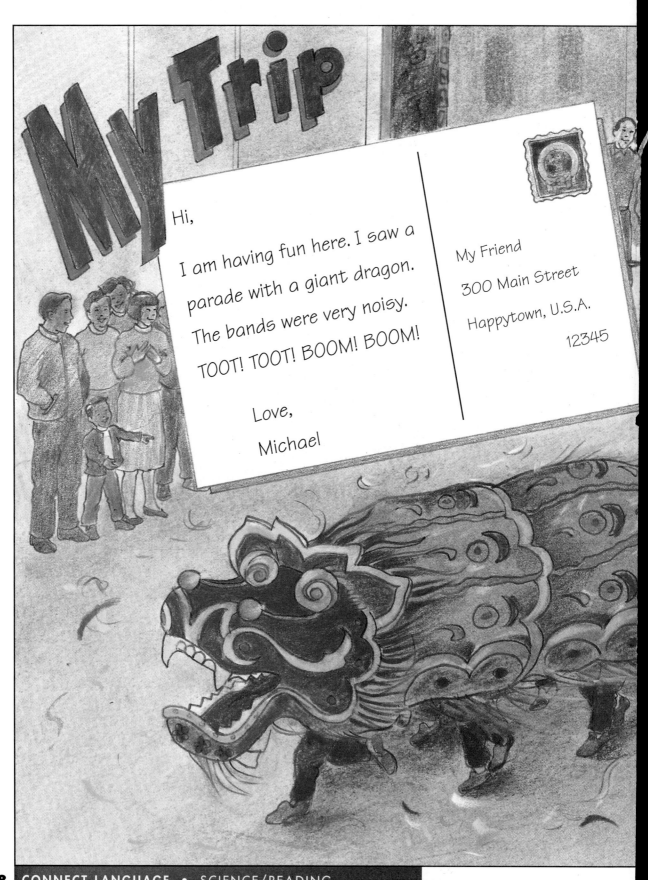

My Trip

Hi,

I am having fun here. I saw a parade with a giant dragon. The bands were very noisy. TOOT! TOOT! BOOM! BOOM!

Love,
Michael

My Friend
300 Main Street
Happytown, U.S.A.
                12345

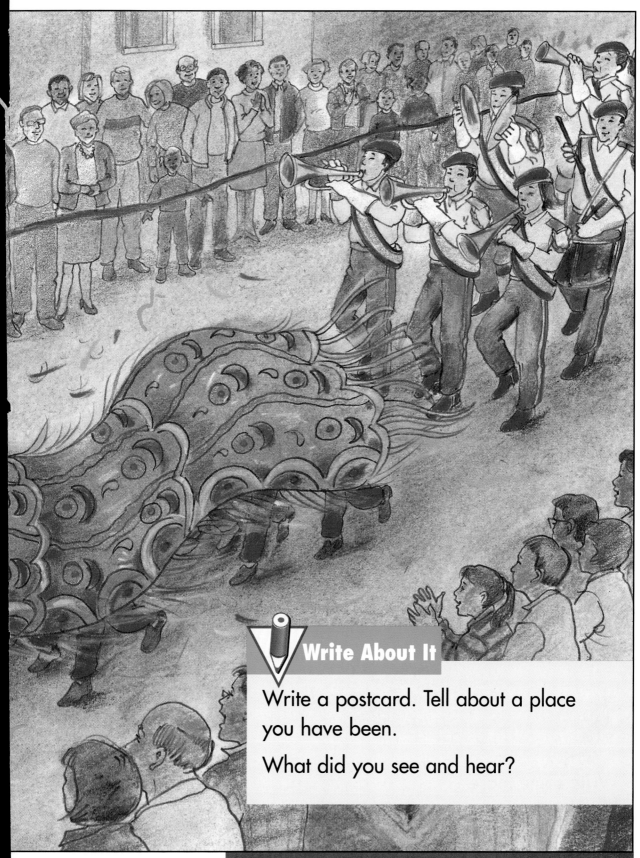

### Write About It

Write a postcard. Tell about a place you have been.

What did you see and hear?

# The Clap and Quiet Poem

The Clap and Quiet Poem

**by Dee Lillegard**

*Clap, clap, clap . . .*

*My hands make noise.*

*Clap, clap, clap . . .*

*Let's hear the boys.*

*Clap, clap, clap . . .*

*Now girls clap too.*

*Clap, clap, clap . . .*

*And now we're through!*

*Quiet hands.*

*Quiet face.*

*Let's have quiet*

*Every place.*

 **Try It Out**

*Shhh . . .*

Write some more
lines for this poem.

# Tell what you learned.

**1.** Name one thing that makes a loud sound. Name one thing that makes a soft sound.

**2.** Can you see better with one eye or with two eyes?

**3.** Draw a picture of a place you have been. Show things you saw and heard. Label your picture.

# Tell what you know.

What are the months of the year?

# The Four Seasons

| January | | | | | | |
|---|---|---|---|---|---|---|
| S | M | T | W | T | F | S |
| 1 | 2 | 3 | 4 | 5 | 6 | 7 |
| 8 | 9 | 10 | 11 | 12 | 13 | 14 |
| 15 | 16 | 17 | 18 | 19 | 20 | 21 |
| 22 | 23 | 24 | 25 | 26 | 27 | 28 |
| 29 | 30 | 31 | | | | |

| February | | | | | | |
|---|---|---|---|---|---|---|
| S | M | T | W | T | F | S |
| | | | 1 | 2 | 3 | 4 |
| 5 | 6 | 7 | 8 | 9 | 10 | 11 |
| 12 | 13 | 14 | 15 | 16 | 17 | 18 |
| 19 | 20 | 21 | 22 | 23 | 24 | 25 |
| 26 | 27 | 28 | | | | |

| March | | | | | | |
|---|---|---|---|---|---|---|
| S | M | T | W | T | F | S |
| | | | 1 | 2 | 3 | 4 |
| 5 | 6 | 7 | 8 | 9 | 10 | 11 |
| 12 | 13 | 14 | 15 | 16 | 17 | 18 |
| 19 | 20 | 21 | 22 | 23 | 24 | 25 |
| 26 | 27 | 28 | 29 | 30 | 31 | |

| April | | | | | | |
|---|---|---|---|---|---|---|
| S | M | T | W | T | F | S |
| | | | | | | 1 |
| 2 | 3 | 4 | 5 | 6 | 7 | 8 |
| 9 | 10 | 11 | 12 | 13 | 14 | 15 |
| 16 | 17 | 18 | 19 | 20 | 21 | 22 |
| 23 / 30 | 24 | 25 | 26 | 27 | 28 | 29 |

| May | | | | | | |
|---|---|---|---|---|---|---|
| S | M | T | W | T | F | S |
| | 1 | 2 | 3 | 4 | 5 | 6 |
| 7 | 8 | 9 | 10 | 11 | 12 | 13 |
| 14 | 15 | 16 | 17 | 18 | 19 | 20 |
| 21 | 22 | 23 | 24 | 25 | 26 | 27 |
| 28 | 29 | 30 | 31 | | | |

| June | | | | | | |
|---|---|---|---|---|---|---|
| S | M | T | W | T | F | S |
| | | | | 1 | 2 | 3 |
| 4 | 5 | 6 | 7 | 8 | 9 | 10 |
| 11 | 12 | 13 | 14 | 15 | 16 | 17 |
| 18 | 19 | 20 | 21 | 22 | 23 | 24 |
| 25 | 26 | 27 | 28 | 29 | 30 | |

| July | | | | | | |
|---|---|---|---|---|---|---|
| S | M | T | W | T | F | S |
| | | | | | | 1 |
| 2 | 3 | 4 | 5 | 6 | 7 | 8 |
| 9 | 10 | 11 | 12 | 13 | 14 | 15 |
| 16 | 17 | 18 | 19 | 20 | 21 | 22 |
| 23 / 30 | 24 / 31 | 25 | 26 | 27 | 28 | 29 |

| August | | | | | | |
|---|---|---|---|---|---|---|
| S | M | T | W | T | F | S |
| | | 1 | 2 | 3 | 4 | 5 |
| 6 | 7 | 8 | 9 | 10 | 11 | 12 |
| 13 | 14 | 15 | 16 | 17 | 18 | 19 |
| 20 | 21 | 22 | 23 | 24 | 25 | 26 |
| 27 | 28 | 29 | 30 | 31 | | |

| September | | | | | | |
|---|---|---|---|---|---|---|
| S | M | T | W | T | F | S |
| | | | | | 1 | 2 |
| 3 | 4 | 5 | 6 | 7 | 8 | 9 |
| 10 | 11 | 12 | 13 | 14 | 15 | 16 |
| 17 | 18 | 19 | 20 | 21 | 22 | 23 |
| 24 | 25 | 26 | 27 | 28 | 29 | 30 |

| October | | | | | | |
|---|---|---|---|---|---|---|
| S | M | T | W | T | F | S |
| 1 | 2 | 3 | 4 | 5 | 6 | 7 |
| 8 | 9 | 10 | 11 | 12 | 13 | 14 |
| 15 | 16 | 17 | 18 | 19 | 20 | 21 |
| 22 | 23 | 24 | 25 | 26 | 27 | 28 |
| 29 | 30 | 31 | | | | |

| November | | | | | | |
|---|---|---|---|---|---|---|
| S | M | T | W | T | F | S |
| | | | 1 | 2 | 3 | 4 |
| 5 | 6 | 7 | 8 | 9 | 10 | 11 |
| 12 | 13 | 14 | 15 | 16 | 17 | 18 |
| 19 | 20 | 21 | 22 | 23 | 24 | 25 |
| 26 | 27 | 28 | 29 | 30 | | |

| December | | | | | | |
|---|---|---|---|---|---|---|
| S | M | T | W | T | F | S |
| | | | | | 1 | 2 |
| 3 | 4 | 5 | 6 | 7 | 8 | 9 |
| 10 | 11 | 12 | 13 | 14 | 15 | 16 |
| 17 | 18 | 19 | 20 | 21 | 22 | 23 |
| 24 / 31 | 25 | 26 | 27 | 28 | 29 | 30 |

# What are the four seasons of the year?

winter

spring

fall

summer

**Talk About It**

Which season do you like best? Why?

# What is it like in each season?

▲ In most places in the U. S., it is colder in **winter.**

▲ It is warmer in **spring.**

▲ It is hotter in **summer.**

▲ It is cooler in **fall.**

**Talk About It**

What season is it now?

What is the weather like where you live?

# What can you do in different weather?

windy

cloudy

sunny

snowy

rainy

# How can you dress for the weather?

◄ What would you wear on a snowy day?

What would you wear ▶ on a rainy day?

◄ What would you wear on a sunny day?

**Draw About It**

What do you like to do when it is sunny? What do you wear?

Draw a picture.

# How does a coat keep you warm?

**Things You Need**

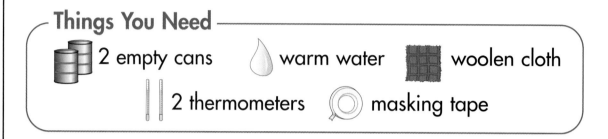

2 empty cans    warm water    woolen cloth

2 thermometers    masking tape

**Follow these steps.**

**1.** Wrap the cloth around one can.
Tape the cloth in place.

**2.** Fill each can with warm water.

**3.** Put a thermometer in each can.

**4.** Measure the temperature
of the water in each can.
Do this every 5 minutes
for 20 minutes.

# Keep a record.

Make a chart like this.

Write the temperature of the water in each can.

|  | temperature of water with cloth | temperature of water without cloth |
|---|---|---|
| at start |  |  |
| after 5 minutes |  |  |
| after 10 minutes |  |  |
| after 15 minutes |  |  |
| after 20 minutes |  |  |

## ❓ Think About It

Which can of water stayed warmer?

How is a cloth around a can like a coat you wear on a cold day?

# Trees and Seasons

How does this apple tree change
with each season?

▲ There are no leaves
in winter.

▲ There are buds and
blossoms in spring.

▲ Leaves and apples
grow in summer.

▲ Apples are picked.
Leaves change colors
in fall.

# Trees in Forests

People like to visit forests in different seasons.

How do people enjoy the forest?

## Word Bank

**gather**

**hike**

**look**

**ski**

## Talk About It

How would you like to spend time in the forest?

# The Good Morning Weather Report

## Good Morning, Chicago!

Here is the weather for this winter day. It is snowy. It is very cold. The temperature is 8 degrees. The wind is blowing hard.

Don't forget to put on your snow boots!

## Good Morning, San Francisco!

Here is the weather for this winter day. It is rainy. The temperature is 55 degrees. The wind is blowing softly.

Don't forget to take along a raincoat and umbrella.

## Good Morning, Miami!

Here is the weather for this winter day. It is sunny. The temperature is 73 degrees. The wind is blowing softly.

Don't forget to take along your sunglasses and a sun hat.

## Good Morning, Dallas!

Here is the weather for this winter day. It is cloudy and cool. The temperature is 35 degrees. The wind is blowing hard.

Don't forget to wear a warm jacket.

### Talk About It

Which place is most like where you live?

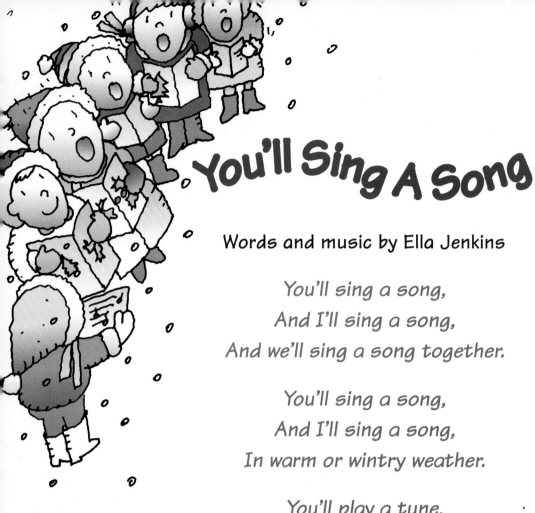

# You'll Sing A Song

**Words and music by Ella Jenkins**

You'll sing a song,
And I'll sing a song,
And we'll sing a song together.

You'll sing a song,
And I'll sing a song,
In warm or wintry weather.

You'll play a tune,
And I'll play a tune,
And we'll play a tune together.

You'll play a tune,
And I'll play a tune,
In warm or wintry weather.

**Try It Out**

Make up new
verses for the song
to sing together.

# Tell what you learned.

**1.** What are the four seasons?

**2.** What are the people doing? What season is it?

**3.** Draw a picture of winter where you live. Show what you are wearing.

# Trees

## Tell what you know.

Who needs trees?

**Talk About It**

What animals live near trees where you live?

# How do people use trees?

▲ People cut down trees for wood.

▲ People burn wood to make heat.

▲ People build things from wood.

### Word Bank

**blocks**

**chairs**

**door**

**floor**

**houses**

**paper**

**pencils**

**toys**

▲ People make paper from wood.

People use wood in many ways.

### Talk About It

Look around. Name other things that are made of wood.

# How can we save trees?

People cut down trees to make paper.

People can **recycle** paper to save trees.

To recycle means to use again.

How do the children recycle the paper?

People can protect trees from fire.

People can plant new trees.

## Talk About It

How can you save paper?

# How are trees alike and different?

Different kinds of trees grow in different places.

Palm trees grow in ▶ warm places.

◀ Willow trees grow in warm and cold places.

Pine trees grow in warm ▶ and cold places.

# How are leaves alike and different?

The leaves of different trees have different shapes.

Collect different kinds of leaves.

Group the leaves that are alike.

How many groups do you have?

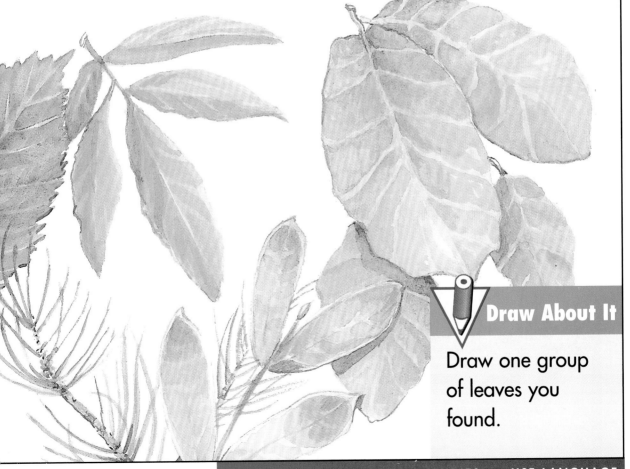

**Draw About It**

Draw one group of leaves you found.

# What do tree seeds do?

Tree seeds are different sizes
and shapes.

All tree seeds are alike in one way.

All tree seeds can grow into
new trees.

# Plant a tree seed.

**Things You Need**

tree seeds  soil  cup

plastic bag  water

**Follow these steps.**

**1.** Fill a cup with soil. Water the soil.

**2.** Plant a tree seed in the soil.

**3.** Cover the cup with a plastic bag.

**4.** Put the cup in a warm, sunny place.

**5.** Add a few drops of water to the soil each day.

**?Think About It**

What will happen to the seed?

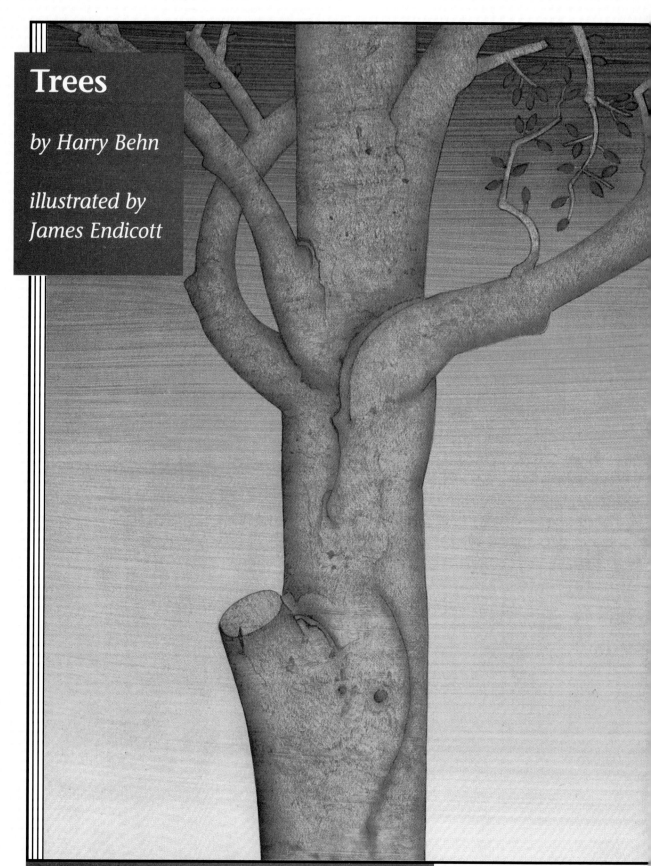

# Trees

*by Harry Behn*

*illustrated by*
*James Endicott*

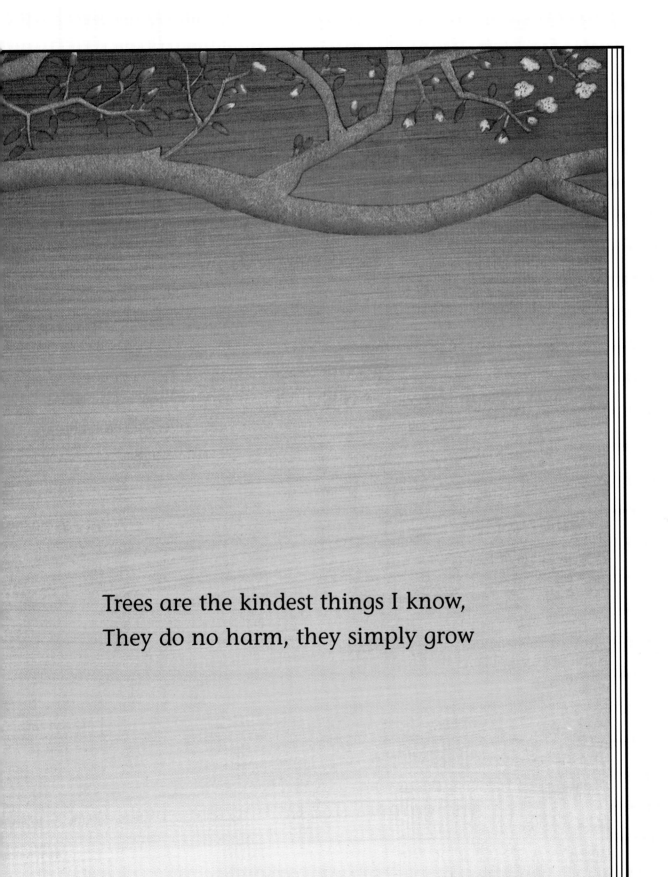

Trees are the kindest things I know,
They do no harm, they simply grow

And spread a shade for sleepy cows,

And gather birds among their boughs.

They give us fruit in leaves above,

And wood to make our houses of,

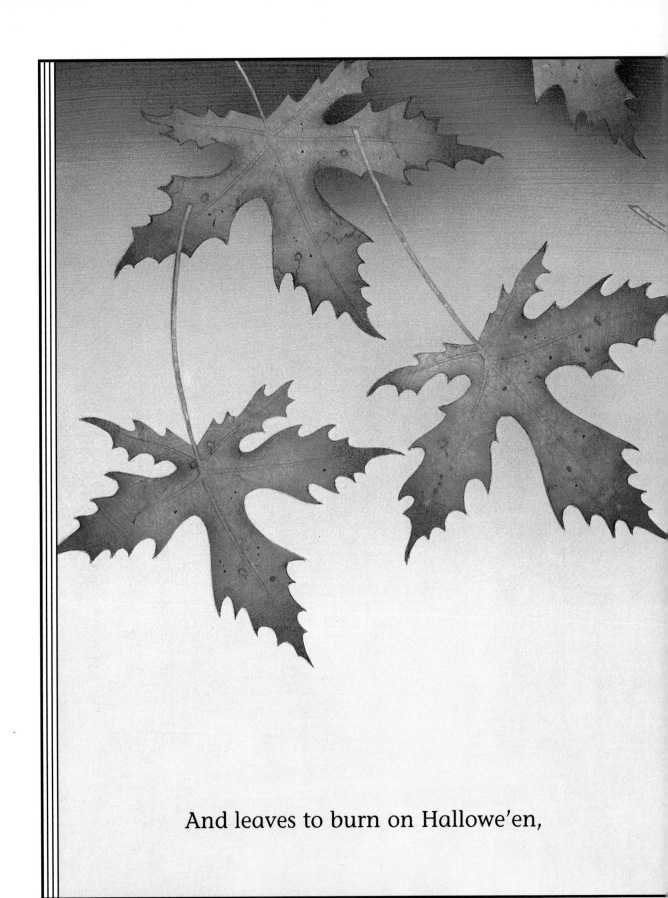

And leaves to burn on Hallowe'en,

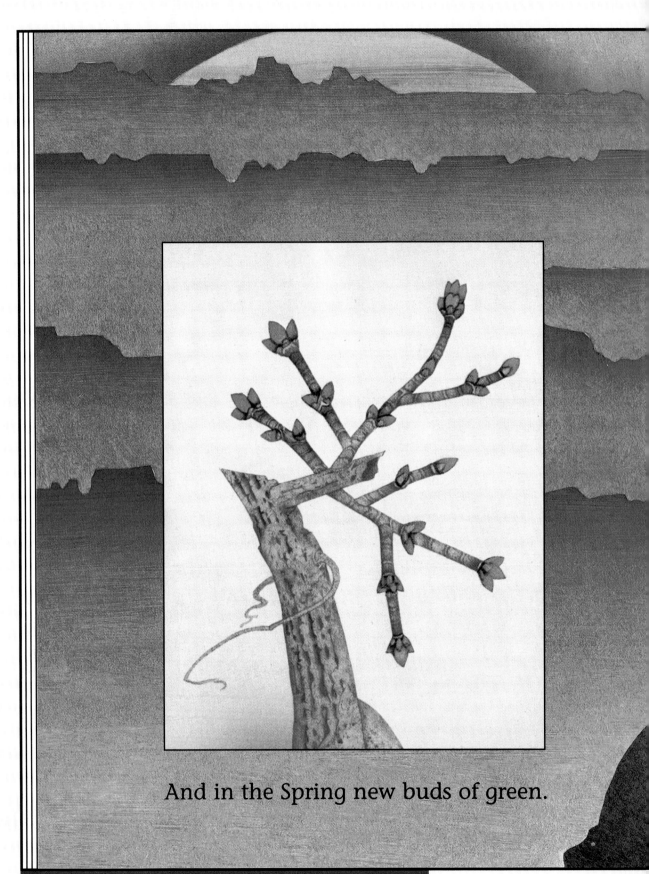

And in the Spring new buds of green.

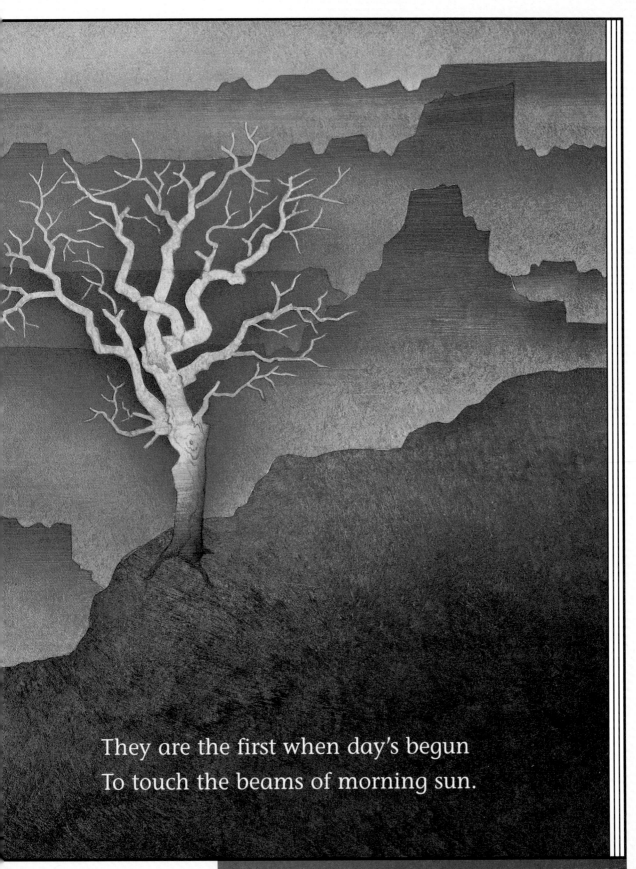

They are the first when day's begun
To touch the beams of morning sun.

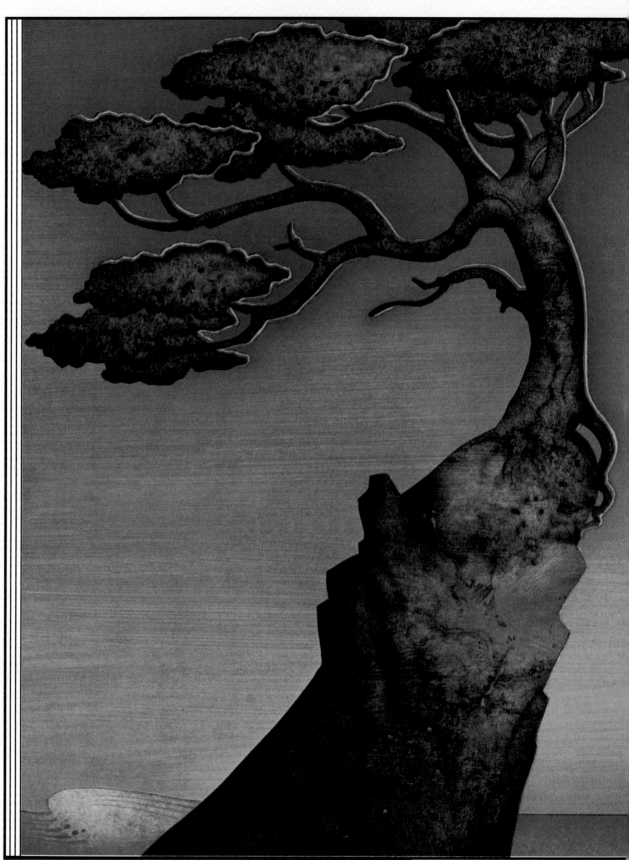

They are the last to hold the light
When evening changes into night,

And when a moon floats on the sky
They hum a drowsy lullaby

Of sleepy children long ago . . .

Trees are the kindest things I know.

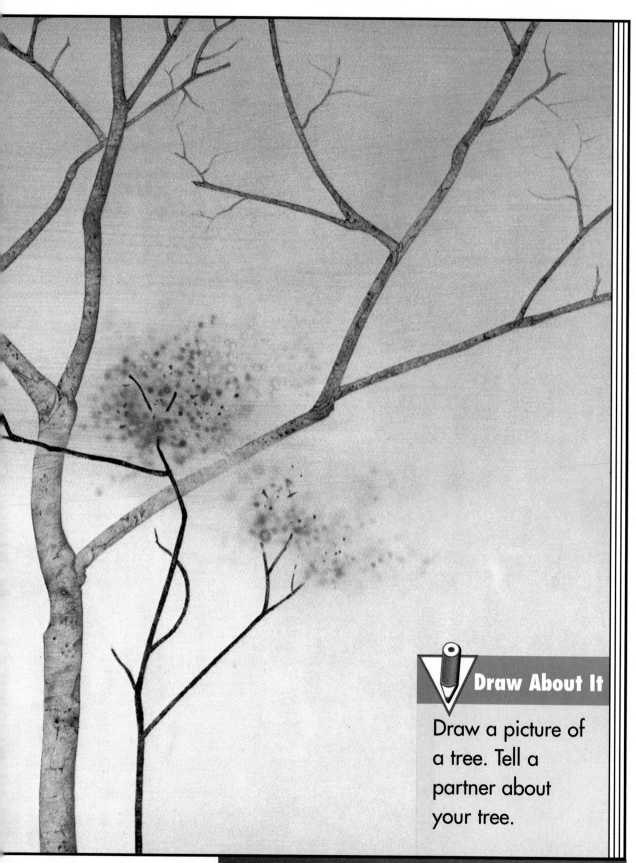

### Draw About It

Draw a picture of a tree. Tell a partner about your tree.

# Shadows

by Leland B. Jacobs

The shadows of bushes
    Are much too small;
They hardly cover
    A child at all.

But the shadows of trees
    Are long and wide,
So that's the place
    Where I like to hide.

If I hide in the bushes,
    Everyone sees
My arms and hands
    Or my legs and knees.

But deep in the shadow
    Of a tree,
Not even the sun
    Can discover me.

## Try It Out

On a sunny day, look at your shadow
in the morning. Look again at noon.
How has it changed?

# Tell what you learned.

**1.** Name two things made from trees.

**2.** How can you help save trees?

**3.** Write what you learned about trees when you read the poem "Trees."

Children's
Reference
Section

# ① Alphabet

Aa

Ee

Bb

Ff

Cc

Gg

Dd

Hh

Ii

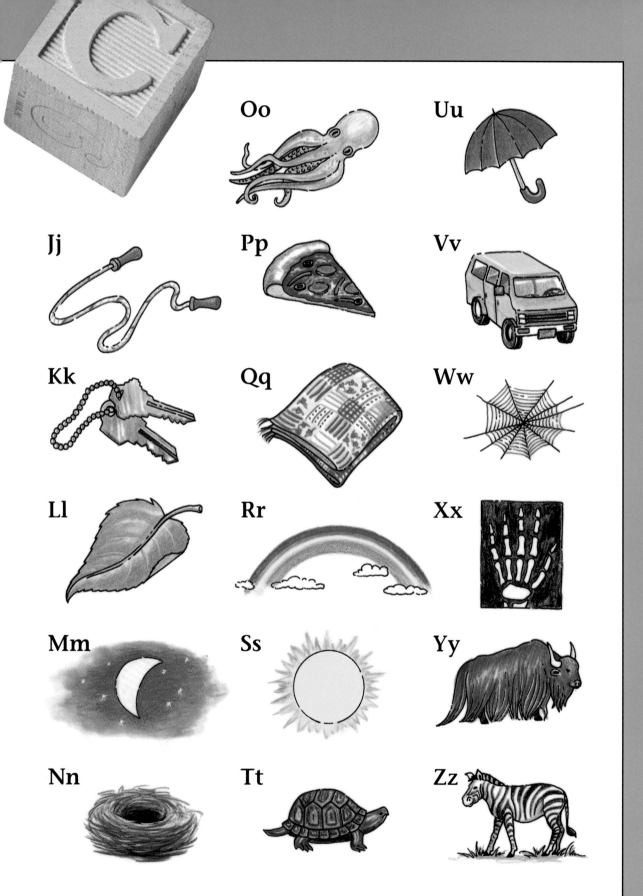

Oo

Uu

Jj

Pp

Vv

Kk

Qq

Ww

Ll

Rr

Xx

Mm

Ss

Yy

Nn

Tt

Zz

# ② Colors and Shapes

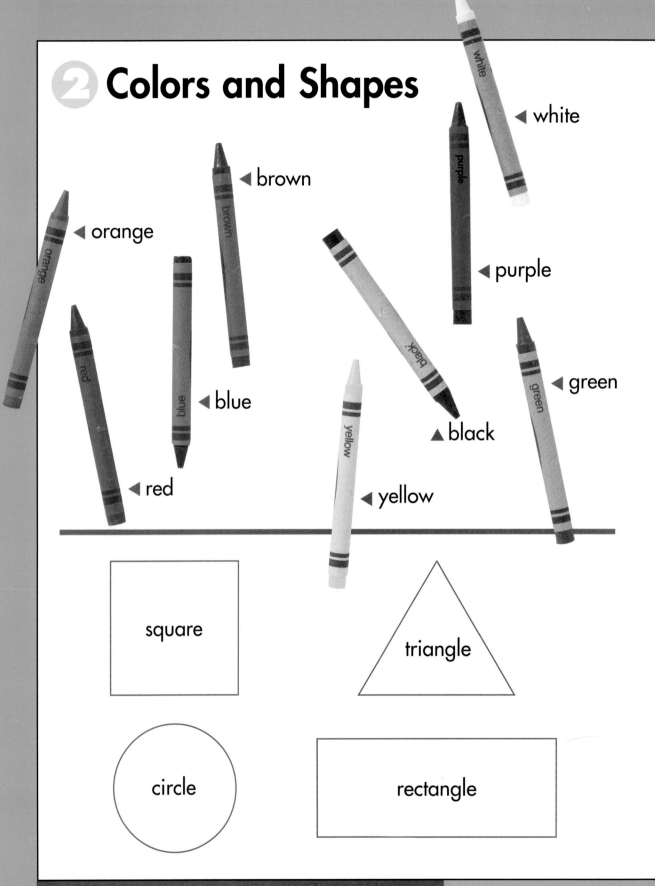

◄ white

◄ brown

◄ orange

◄ purple

◄ blue

◄ purple

◄ green

▲ black

◄ red

◄ yellow

square

triangle

circle

rectangle

# ③ Numbers

**1** one

**2** two

**3** three

**4** four

**5** five

**6** six

**7** seven

**8** eight

**9** nine

**10** ten

# ④ Days and Seasons

| November | | | | | | |
|---|---|---|---|---|---|---|
| SUNDAY | MONDAY | TUESDAY | WEDNESDAY | THURSDAY | FRIDAY | SATURDAY |
|  | 1 | 2 | 3 | 4 | 5 | 6 |
| 7 | 8 | 9 | 10 | 11 | 12 | 13 |
| 14 | 15 | 16 | 17 | 18 | 19 | 20 |
| 21 | 22 | 23 | 24 | 25 | 26 | 27 |
| 28 | 29 | 30 |  |  |  |  |

days of week

seasons

winter

fall

summer

spring

# ⑤ Body Parts

head

ear

eye

nose

mouth

finger

arm

hand

leg

toe

foot

# 6 Senses

▲ see

▲ hear

▲ touch

◄ smell

▲ taste